For 21 years Dr James A. Simpson was minister of Dornoch Cathedral in the Scottish Highlands. During his time there he not only served as captain of the Royal Dornoch Golf Club, but wrote many books, some of which topped Scottish bestseller charts. Dr Simpson is a regular contributor to magazines and newspapers, at home and abroad. He is also much in demand as an after-dinner speaker.

In 1992 he was appointed chaplain to the Queen in Scotland. Two years later he was elected Moderator of the General Assembly of the Church of Scotland.

Dr Simpson has long believed that in any lecture, discussion or debate a little comic relief does no harm, no matter how serious the topic may be.

By the same author

Uncommon Sense

...and comic nonsense

James A. Simpson

Steve Savage
LONDON AND EDINBURGH

Steve Savage Publishers Ltd
The Old Truman Brewery
91 Brick Lane
LONDON
E1 6QL

www.savagepublishers.com

First published in Great Britain by Steve Savage Publishers Ltd 2016

Copyright © James A. Simpson 2016

ISBN: 978-1-904246-45-9

Typeset by Steve Savage Publishers Ltd
Printed and bound by SRP Press, Exeter

Contents

Dedication

*To the congregation of Dornoch Cathedral whom I
was privileged to serve for 21 years, and to the
members of the Royal Dornoch Golf Club who this
year celebrate golf having been played on the
Dornoch links for 400 years.*

Acknowledgements

*The author would like to thank The Society of Authors as the
Literary Representative of the Estate of John Masefield for
permission to quote from his poem 'Cargoes'.*

*I also wish to acknowledge a number of individuals who
have helped make this book possible. Lynne McNeil, the editor of*
Life and Work, *our national church magazine, for
encouraging me to write a monthly article, and for granting me
permission to use excerpts from some of these articles. Peter
Thomson and Bob Sloan, two highly respected friends, who
kindly agreed to read the manuscript and make helpful
comments. My publisher Steve Savage who continues to be
enormously supportive, and my wife Helen, who for 56 years
has been my greatest friend, encourager and critic.*

PROLOGUE

Among life's many mysteries,
I have often wondered why
We designate as 'common' sense
A trait in short supply
A.W. Engelhardt

The parish of *Dull*, near where I live in Perthshire, was recently linked with the town of *Boring* in Oregon! Though both Dull and Boring are located in scenically beautiful parts of the world, I would not have wanted, for obvious reasons, to be an author or minister in either of these parishes.

"The author's purpose," said Joseph Conrad, "is by the power of the written word to make people hear, make them feel and above all *make people see*." I believe it is no different with after-dinner speakers and preachers. The best way to avoid being boring is by painting word pictures and telling relevant stories, by giving hearers and readers a sight track as well as a sound track. This has certainly often helped me get a half-nelson on what have sometimes been very slippery audiences! What we say and write lasts longer in the memory when presented in the form of a story. Three of the finest story tellers, Aesop, Jesus of Nazareth and Hans Christian Andersen used stories not only to teach truths in a simple understandable way, but to change people's thinking. They knew that stories help people see what they would not have seen as clearly if communicated in more abstract language. The response of readers or listeners to a good story is often to nod their heads and say, "I now better understand what you are saying."

Few human traits are more important than *Uncommon Sense*, or what Scots sometimes call 'gumption'. This rare trait, as Engelhardt calls it, helps those who have it, to distinguish what matters most in life from what does not matter all that much, the primary from the secondary, the essential from the incidental. In the chapters that follow, by means of numerous stories, stories that fascinated and startled me, that sometimes caused a lump to form in my throat and bring a tear to my eye, stories that made me smile and laugh, that provided insights into human nature and its propensity to rise to great heights and sink to great depths, I have sought to shed further light on what I mean by uncommon sense. Though readers of these numerous and humorous anecdotes might conclude that I am in my '*anecdotage*', hopefully no reader will describe what I have written as dull or boring!

As with my previous books, the royalties from this book will go to support Cystic Fibrosis Research, a disease from which Sally, my much loved oldest granddaughter suffered.

James A. Simpson

Too Busy and Too Fast

An American visitor once asked a Mexican fisherman how long his fine catch had taken. When told that it had not taken all that long, the American asked why then did he not spend longer fishing? When the fisherman explained that he had caught enough to support his family, the American inquired what he did the rest of his day. "My wife and I have a siesta. We enjoy leisure activities with our children. I also sometimes play my guitar with friends." "But," said the American businessman, "if you were to spend more time at sea each day, you could soon buy a fleet of boats, open a processing factory and ultimately sell a thriving business." When the fisherman asked "But what then?" the American said, "Well you could retire and live the kind of life you want." "But I do that now," said the puzzled Mexican.

Early one December Seth Myers, an American comedian, told on television how some superstores were delivering freshly cut Christmas trees to the purchaser's home. For a few dollars more, those delivering the tree would erect and decorate the tree. They would also wrap presents. By doing this, Seth Myers said, the store staff will experience the joy that busy parents no longer have time for!

Work lovers who make time to relax and be with their families, who have other sources of enjoyment and satisfaction outwith their work, are mostly happier people than work addicts. During my years as a parish minister, I often talked with people who were terminally ill. Not one of them ever expressed regret that they had not spent more time at the office. But many said wistfully that they wished they had invested more time in relationships, and doing things with their children.

❧

In the days before mobile phones and satellite navigation, a lady got seriously lost on her way to visit a friend who had moved house. Thirty minutes after her planned arrival time, she was speeding through the city suburbs, when she saw a police car in her mirror, its blue light flashing. Pulling over, she apologised to the policeman: "I know I was speeding, but I have been lost for forty minutes and I cannot find the address I am looking for." "I am sorry about that, ma'am, but what made you think that hurrying would help you find it?"

The temptation is strong in many spheres of life to go faster and faster without asking why? One doctor described the continual rush of modern life as 'time sickness'. Irritability, ulcers, heart attacks and nervous breakdowns are often the result. I find it significant that the Chinese word for busy is composed of two characters, one for 'heart' and the other for 'killing'. When we make ourselves so busy that we are always rushing around, trying to get countless things done, we kill something vital in ourselves, and we smother the quiet common sense of our heart. We all need to learn that there is a time to slow down, lay down the briefcase and laptop, stop the car and get out and admire the view.

Deeds not Years

The vital distinction between length and quality of life is hinted at in a remark of D. H. Lawrence. "Poor old Queen

Victoria had length of days, but Emily Brontë had life." The poet Ben Jonson expressed the same truth beautifully:

> *It is not living long an oak*
> *Three hundred years*
> *To fall a log at last, dry, bald and sere.*
> *A lily of a day is fairer far in May.*
> *Although it fall and die that night,*
> *It was the plant and flower of light.*

The poet Keats died at 26, Burns at 37, but not before leaving poetry the centuries will not quickly forget. Schubert died at 31, Mozart at 35, but not before giving the world music that time will never silence. How swift were the careers of Francis of Assisi, Edith Cavell and Martin Luther King – great flashes of light that the world has not quickly forgotten. By this world's calendar, Jesus' life was short, but what an unparalleled influence for good he exerted.

> *We live in deeds, not years; in thoughts not breaths;*
> *In feelings, not in figures on a dial.*
> *We should count time by heart-throbs. He most lives,*
> *Who thinks most – feels the noblest – acts the best.*

The real value of a life consists not in its duration but its donation.

Walking

Today in Britain, recreational walking is the most popular leisure activity. Walkers in England hike over many new trails, as well as some ancient Roman paths. Some of Scotland's oldest hill walks were built at the time of the

Jacobite rebellion to allow soldiers to move more quickly over the rugged landscape. The silver lining to the dark cloud that Dr Beeching cast over our railway network in the 1960s is that today many disused railway tracks are greatly enjoyed by ramblers.

Walkers have not only made and continue to make a considerable contribution to the economy, they have brought about many needed reforms. It was walkers who succeeded in ending the segregation of black and white people on American buses. Under the leadership of Martin Luther King, the black people of Montgomery, Alabama, refused to ride the city buses, no matter how far they lived from their work, or how inclement the weather. Dr King eloquently summarised their protest: "They came to see that it was ultimately more honourable to walk the streets in dignity than to ride the buses in humiliation."

❧

Many novelists, poets and song-writers have claimed that walking enhanced their creativity. "Sure by Tummel and Loch Rannoch and Lochaber I will go" – not by car, bus or train, but on foot. It was while out walking in the Lake District that Wordsworth saw 'a crowd, a host of golden daffodils, fluttering and dancing in the breeze'. After one of these walks he wrote of that 'blessed mood, in which the heavy and weary weight of this world is lightened.'

❧

Early on in my ministry, I was signed off with stress, caused by working punishing hours and trying to fill every minute with sixty seconds' worth of distance run. In those days, outsiders watching me might well have concluded I regarded relaxation as a vice. Long walks along back roads were part of the therapy prescribed. Even bracing hikes in winter nourished a deeper appreciation of all things bright and beautiful, the snow transforming common trees into works of art. Walking helped me see things more in perspective. I found myself more at ease with the world.

At the end of a walk along a river bank, Robert Burns wrote:

> *Ye banks and braes o' bonnie Doon*
> *How can ye bloom sae fresh and fair?*
> *How can ye chant ye little birds*
> *And I sae weary, fu' o' care?*
>
> *Oft have I roved by bonnie Doon*
> *To see the rose and woodbine twine,*
> *And ilka bird sang o' its love*
> *And fondly sae did I o' mine.*

In our highly pressurised working environment, walking is good not only for our coronary arteries and physical well-being, but also, by lessening anxieties, good for our sanity. Walkers do not have to choose their favourite among the seasons. All they have to do is to rejoice in the beauty of their differences.

Friends

As a young man Robert Burns went to Irvine, to learn the trade of flax dressing. There he was befriended by a dubious character concerning whom Burns later said, "His friendship did me a mischief." In every community there are such people. But thankfully there are also those whose friendship ennobles. I think of the influence which the friendship of the Anglican priest Father Huddleston had on the young Desmond Tutu, and countless others in South Africa. I think also of the transforming influence of the gracious Louise Whitfield on her husband, the steel baron, Andrew Carnegie. No less significant are the changes wrought by caring teachers and dedicated youth leaders on troubled youngsters. The secret of many lives has been that of finding the right friend at the right time.

Shirley Temple gained immense fame and fortune at an early age, but unfortunately this resulted in her never having close childhood friends. What a loss. In an isolating and disjointed world, friends are, at every stage of life, an indispensable ingredient of a full and happy life. "It is not our level of prosperity," said the Russian writer Solzhenitsyn, "that makes for happiness, but the way we look at the world and the kinship of heart with heart."

For the ancient Greeks, "Summer and Winter" symbolised true friendship. They knew true friends share not only our bright days but our dark days. Whereas an acquaintance wants to share our prosperity, real friends insist on sharing our adversity. Like phosphorescence, such friendships glow brightest when the world around goes dark.

The most durable prize which my seriously ill granddaughter Sally gained from her years at university was not her first-class honours degree, but the friendship of a most caring young man who became her husband, and the friendship of many university girl-friends who supported her wonderfully through her final terminal illness. Sally had far better friends than Job ever had.

Glory Be

An Irish poet exclaimed, "What can we cry but *Glory Be*, when God breaks out in an apple tree." It was in the spring of 1976 that I moved from Glasgow to Dornoch, an area described by the Countryside Commission as the area of greatest natural beauty on the East Coast of Scotland. In the weeks that followed, as I walked the beach or played the golf course, breathing in the fresh sea air and observing the riot of colour in the yellow banks of gorse, I often exclaimed, "Glory Be." It was no different later in the year when I was privileged to enjoy the beauty of 'the purple headed mountains and the rivers running by.' "Earth's crammed with heaven," wrote Elizabeth Barrett Browning, "and every common bush afire with God." Then she added, "But only he who sees takes off his shoes."

The week prior to the British Amateur Golf Championship being played at Royal Dornoch, I asked Duffy Waldorf, the leading American contender, how his practising was going. "I have not really started practising yet," he said. "I am still soaking up the scenery." It is marvellous scenery, but just as, in the Caribbean, locals seldom comment on the temperature of the warm water or the cloudless skies, so there are those in the County of Sutherland who have grown so accustomed to the incredible beauty all around them, that they seldom stop and marvel at it.

Most of us, if asked to paint a tree, would paint the trunk black or brown. But in fact tree trunks are just about every colour except black or brown. They are a mixture of grey, yellow, green and, purple. It was a keen observer of nature who coined the word 'saunter' from the French words, 'sainte terre', meaning 'holy land.' Going for a walk was for him a pilgrimage through the *holy land* that lay all around him. Within a few miles of his home, he observed more of interest than many do on a world tour.

Perhaps we should measure life, not by the number of breaths taken, but by the number of moments when our breath is taken away, when the air is drawn out of our lungs in some such exclamation as 'Look' or 'Glory Be.'

Humour – A Sign of Sanity

Life is not just about work and duty. It is also about relaxation and fun. It concerns me that many think of 'religious folk' as grimly serious people, rather than people with a smile on their faces and a great deal of kindness in their hearts. This also concerned Charles Spurgeon, one of the outstanding English preachers of the 19th century. "I don't believe in going about like some monks whom I saw in Rome, who salute each other in sepulchral tones and convey the pleasant information, *Brothers we must die!* To this lively salutation each lively brother of the order replies, *Yes brother, we must die!* I was glad to be assured upon such good authority that all these lazy fellows are about to die. It is about the best thing they could do."

I am glad that highly respected 20th-century Christians like C. S. Lewis, Donald Soper, Harry Secombe and Tom Fleming all practised a religion that had a deep and joyous laugh in it, for without humour, religion can quickly become a prey to arrogance and intolerance. Some of the most dangerous people in our world today are fanatical humourless

Muslims, Jews and Christians who are certain they alone are right. A sense of humour can protect us from delusions concerning our own righteousness and superior virtues. When we lose that capacity, we begin to lose our footing. As long as we can laugh at ourselves, there is hope for us and the things we hold dear. Kindly humour is in fact one of the few forms of contagion that we can rightly call a blessing.

❧

Above the abbey door where Sir Walter Scott is buried, there is the uplifting inscription, "Sweeten bitter things with gentle laughter." Despite a turbulent and tragic history, the Jewish people did just that. They developed a genius for comedy. Jewish humour expressed a heroic defiance in the face of crushing defeats, a nobility of spirit that refused to permit an oppressor or a prejudiced society to have the last word. A Jewish proverb says, "When you are hungry, sing, when you are hurt, laugh." Many Jews found sanity through humour.

Jewish humour is often self-deprecating. Jews love poking fun at themselves and their idiosyncracies. They tell of a Jewish grandmother who was watching her grandchild playing on the beach when a huge wave came and took him out to sea. "Please God," she pleaded, "save my only grandson." At that moment a big wave came and washed the boy back on to the beach, unharmed. She looked up to heaven and said with a scowl, "He had a hat!"

There is also a lovely story of an orthodox Jew whose daughter was to be married on the Sabbath. When the bride asked her Dad to shave for her wedding, he said. "I cannot. It is the Sabbath." "Father, please do it for me," she pleaded. When again he said he could not because it was the Sabbath, the daughter said, "Father, at least go and ask the rabbi and see if he will give you permission to shave." Seeing how upset she was, the father agreed to do this. When he called on the rabbi, he found him standing in front of a mirror shaving. "Rabbi," the father said, "may I shave today for my daughter's wedding?" "No," the rabbi replied, "it is the Sabbath." "But," said the father, "you have shaved yourself." "Yes," said the rabbi, "because I did not ask anyone's permission."

The Healing Power of Laughter

Laughter is for me a sign of mental health. If too long a period goes by without it, I begin to analyse my life. Am I too busy, too stressed? The Rev. Doyne Michie believed that laughter is a tranquilliser with many beneficial side-effects. As well as being a respected American minister, he was also an excellent magician and entertainer. In his student days he had become interested in performing 'magic tricks'. During his years as an army chaplain, he sometimes took along a few tricks when he visited seriously wounded soldiers in hospital. Seeing a smile light up their faces, and often hearing a faint laugh, he became convinced some kind of dynamic was at work, that kindly mirth can be a powerful instrument for overcoming melancholy.

During his own recovery from a heart attack, he further experienced the dynamics of laughter therapy. Determined to have some fun in hospital he persuaded his wife to bring him a deck of cards and his 'multiplying rabbit' trick. The effect such fun had on his own recovery, and on his fellow patients in the cardiac unit, further convinced him, and many of the hospital staff, of the medical benefits of laughter therapy, and the truth of what the writer of the

Book of Proverbs said thousands of years before, that "a merry heart doeth good like a medicine".

On leaving hospital, Doyne offered his "Ministry of Laughter" to the infirm, the elderly in hospitals, hospices and care homes, and to health care professionals. Hospital chaplains often contacted him. He recalled one phoning him about a woman who had sunk into deep depression on being informed that she had cancer. At the end of Doyne's visit, the nurse who was with him said, "I noticed that even though you did not know her, you touched her!" She was referring to his rabbit trick, in which little sponge baby bunnies mysteriously jumped from his hand into the lady's, which he had gently held. Her ensuing smile and laugh not only lit up her face, but helped transform her approach to her illness.

In the children's hospital in Atlanta, near to where the Rev. Michie lived, his laughter therapy approach worked its magic as he visited young patients, many of whom, being far from home, were very anxious. A few magic tricks, balloon animals, and a lot of hearty laughs helped reduce their anxiety levels. In a talk which he gave about fighting illness with laughter, he said, "It just may be that laughter is one of God's great gifts to us. I personally have no hesitation in thinking of what I am trying to do as a 'Ministry of Laughter.'"

No Laughing Matter

Peter Dobereiner, the golf writer, said that what sets the truly great golfers apart from the rest, is that they lack a sense of humour. Old Tom Morris, he said, was a man of many virtues, but a sense of humour was not one of them. He criticised the five times Open Champion Harry Vardon

21

for being sour, and James Braid for being dour. Though Ben Hogan came as close as anyone has ever done to achieving complete mastery over the golf ball, there was nothing remotely light-hearted about him.

Dobereiner's observation about these early Open Champions is however far too sweeping a generalisation. When a gushy newspaper reporter told Phil Mickelson, "You are spectacular. Your name is synonymous with the game of golf. You really know your way round the course. What is your secret?" Mickelson replied, "The holes are numbered!"

When Roger Maltbie was asked before the final round of one of the Majors what he would have to shoot to win the tournament, he replied, "The rest of the field." The brilliant Puerto Rican golfer Chi Chi Rodriguez, who was inducted into the World Golf Hall of Fame, was born into a poor Puerto Rican family. Speaking of his boyhood, he often joked that John Daly drove a golf ball further than he went on holiday. Before his very first round in the Masters, he drank a bottle of rum to calm his nerves. At the end of the round Chi Chi, with a big smile on his face, told a reporter, "I shot the happiest 83 of my life!" Dr Pivnick, an American visitor to Dornoch with whom I once golfed, told me of playing with the inimitable, fun-loving Chi Chi. The game finished at the 17th. On the tee of the par 3 18th , Chi Chi said to the young man who had been involved in the game, "If you give me a free throw at this hole, I will give you two strokes and play you for \$20." The young man, being a low handicap golfer, readily accepted the challenge. Rifling his tee shot on to the green, a smile of satisfaction lit up the young man's face. But when they reached the green Chi Chi, whose ball was slightly nearer the hole, used his free throw to hurl the young man's ball out of bounds! No money actually changed hands, just a gift from Chi Chi of new signed balls to replace the lost one.

❧

What a fun loving golfer Lee Trevino also was. When a spectator asked Lee if it concerned him that Jim Dent, an incredibly long hitting golfer, was airmailing him by 50 yards off the tee, he said, "Not at all. He does not always have the right zip code." Once when he was paired with Tony Jacklin in the World Match Play championship, Tony said to Lee at the start, "I don't want to talk today." "That's fine," said Trevino with a smile on his face. "You listen. I'll talk. We are going to be out here for four hours. If we keep our mouths shut for that length of time, we will both get bad breath!"

❧

Few professional golfers have had a finer sense of humour than David Feherty and Peter Alliss, both former Ryder Cup players and now distinguished golf commentators. Their commentaries are always a lovely blend of seriousness and humour. I recall Peter Alliss describing the 65-year-old Gary Player as he walked on to Royal Lytham's last green in the 2001 Open, "Here he comes…the Queen Mother of golf. All he needs is a couple of corgis."

The Laugh Shall Be First

A group of students, having read the sentence, "Men can wear their hair, with or without a parting, unless they are bald", were then shown an alternative version of this sentence, "There are three ways a man can wear his hair:

parted, unparted and departed". The students recalled the humorous version far longer than the straightforward one.

❧

At a team building conference, the co-ordinator divided those present into two groups – men in one group and women in the other. Having written on the board, "A woman without her man is nothing", he then asked the groups to punctuate it correctly. The men wrote: "A woman, without her man, is nothing." The women wrote: "A woman: without her, man is nothing."

❧

Advertisers are well aware how humour increases the attention of viewers to the message hopefully being communicated. Were this not so, advertisers would never have a dog selling insurance or a frog selling beer or a meerkat selling cinema tickets.

❧

A plumber who had been called to sort leaking pipes said to the lady of the house, "It is even worse than I expected. Sorting this mess will put me in a higher tax bracket!"

❧

A young man who at a dance had met an attractive nurse who worked in the local hospital, called one evening at the hospital, hoping to see her. When the lady at reception asked him what he wanted, he said. "I would like to see Nurse Brown. I am her brother." "I am delighted to meet you," said the receptionist. "I'm her mother!"

❧

In the picturesque West Highland village of Plockton, an Eng-lishman was surprised to see a Bed and Breakfast called 'Nessun Dorma', for the English translation is "None shall sleep."

Two American friends from Richmond, Virginia were keen to spend a few days playing the Royal Dornoch golf course. When they asked me how best to get from Inverness Airport to Dornoch, they accepted my suggestion that I would get the local taxi-driver John Gordon to pick them up at the airport. On arriving at the Royal Golf Hotel they asked John what they owed him." "Look," said John, "why don't you just pay me when I take you back to the airport?" "But," said Bob Scott, "what would happen if we died before then?" "Oh," said John, "don't worry about that; I am also the local funeral director!"

🌸

Johnston Mackay, the former Head of Religious Broadcasting in Scotland, and John Fitzimmons, a highly respected Glasgow priest, were one day walking along the shores of the Lake of Galilee in connection with a programme they were working on about the Lake. As they walked they noticed a sign which said, "No Swimming." Later they saw another sign "No Jumping" which had obviously been erected to stop people diving. Turning to Johnston, Father Fitzimmons said, "Has it ever occurred to you that Jesus would have to walk on the water because it seems to be the only thing you are allowed to do here."

🌸

A rural minister tells of receiving a letter, inside which there was an advert about a church that was vacant. The advert described a strong vital city congregation with a great preaching and musical tradition. At the foot of the advert were penned the words "Apply now." At first he felt flattered. There being, however, no indication as to who had sent it, he looked at the envelope – to discover it had been posted locally!

❧

A newly appointed member of the House of Lords once asked Disraeli what course in public speaking he should take to qualify himself for gaining the ear of the House. "Have you a graveyard near your house?" Disraeli asked. When 'yes' was his reply, Disraeli said, "Then I would recommend you visit it early in the morning and practise speaking to the tombstones."

❧

A new teacher was seen one day standing outside his classroom with his forehead pressed firmly against a locker. The headmaster who was passing heard the teacher mutter, "How did you get yourself into this?" Knowing that he had been assigned a difficult class, the headmaster tried to offer moral support. "Are you OK?" Lifting his head the teacher replied, "I'll be fine as soon as I get this kid out of his locker."

❧

A Glasgow lady tells how when her washing machine broke down, she ordered a new one. The two men who delivered the replacement machine agreed to remove the old one. As they took it out of the utility room, she told them that she had had it for 23 years, and felt it was like parting with a member of the family. "In that case," said one of the men, "perhaps you would like a few minutes alone together before we cart it off."

❧

The day after Margaret Thatcher announced outside Downing Street, with her husband Denis standing behind her, that "Today we have become a grandmother," a young conservative MP rose in the House of Commons and proposed that the House should move a motion of congratulation to the Prime Minister on becoming a grandmother. Immediately the satirical Labour MP, Dennis Skinner, rose to his feet. "Mr Speaker, I am prepared to second that motion, but can I add that I hope the baby will become as good a crawler as the person who has proposed this motion!"

An Edinburgh driver visiting Glasgow noticed on the overhead gantry the flashing sign, "Keep your distance." Turning to his travelling companion, who was a Glaswegian, he said, "Whatever happened to Glasgow's legendary friendliness?"

When a shortish chap was overheard saying to a very tall woman in a Glasgow bar, "Do you play basketball?" she inquired, "Do you play mini-golf?"

When the golf professional began the lesson by saying "Let's first just go through the motions without hitting the ball", his pupil said, "But that is precisely the difficulty I am trying to overcome."

When a businessman told his colleague he felt sure he knew his daughter, but could not put a face to her, his colleague apologised, saying "I really ought to carry photographs of my family around with me." "Yes," said the businessman, "but you don't want to see them every time you open your wallet, for I am sure that is exactly what happens at home."

When Lana, who had a habit of driving very fast, was pulled over by a traffic policeman, she asked innocently, "Was I driving too fast?" "No," said the policeman, "it is just that you were flying too low!"

When Laura's grandmother stopped taking her usual walk along the canal, Laura asked her why. She explained that Laura's mother had told her there was a psychopath along that route. Later Laura found out that her mother had actually said, "cycle-path".

A group of fat people, determined to fight discrimination, criticised the use of the term 'overweight'. They said it implied a 'right weight' that fat people had failed to make. They wanted to be called 'total people', and to be thought of in terms of wholeness. They referred to 'thin people' as being 'not all there!' They also claimed to have a 'broad base of support'.

An elderly couple went one morning for breakfast to a restaurant where a highly publicised "Senior Special Breakfast" comprised two eggs, bacon, sausage, potato rissoles, toast and as much coffee as you wanted, all for £3.99. When the waitress asked if they wanted the Senior Special, the wife said, "Sounds good, but I don't want the eggs." "Oh," said the waitress, "then I will have to charge you £4.50, for you are ordering a la carte." "You mean," said her husband, "that my wife will have to pay more for not taking the eggs." When the waitress replied that that was the case, his wife said,

"Well just give me the special breakfast." When the waitress then asked how she would like her eggs, she said, "Raw in the shell." She took the two eggs home and baked a cake!

❀

A man tells how one night he read out a newspaper advertisement to his daughter who was not working all that hard at trying to find a summer job. The advert had been inserted by a local pensioner who was looking for someone to do some light housekeeping. "But," said his daughter, "I know nothing about lighthouses."

❀

Suffering from chest pains, a man went to the hospital to have an ECG. After the test he asked the nurse if everything seemed OK, but she said that she did not know. He would have to wait for the doctor to read the tracing. "But surely you must have some idea," he insisted. "All I know is that if there is a straight line, we're in trouble."

❀

There is nothing harder on the shins than the game of soccer, unless of course the game of bridge.

❀

A lawyer was overheard saying to a colleague, "I believe a man is innocent until he runs out of money."

❀

You cannot put your foot down if you have not a leg to stand on.

❀

A housing development is where councils cut down all the trees and then name the streets after them.

❀

Poster in a slimming clinic. "Join the fight against hazardous waists."

✿

On hearing a female colleague say she had just turned 30, a man was heard to mutter, "She must have made a U-turn somewhere."

✿

If swimming is good for the figure, how do you explain the whale?

✿

If you give some reporters a few facts they will draw their own confusions.

✿

Drive-in banking was invented so that new cars could see their real owners.

✿

A race-horse is an animal that can take several thousand people for a ride at the same time.

✿

Infants have been described as the 'Wet set', neurotics as the 'Fret set', horse-racing fans as the 'Bet set', the ultra rich as the 'Jet set' and most of us as the 'Debt set'.

Gently Scan Your Brother Man

A favourite story of mine concerns two men who were crossing a field in Western Canada. When a bull suddenly came charging towards them, one of them ran and climbed a tree. The other ran and hid in a little cave, in a rocky part of the field. The bull finally quietened down. When the man in the cave reappeared, the bull charged again. Not surprisingly he quickly retreated into the cave. Shortly after the bull had again settled, the man appeared again with the same result. The third time this happened, the man in the tree got frustrated and shouted to his companion, "For goodness sake, stay in the cave until the bull wanders to the other end of the field, and then we can both make a dash for it." Back came the reply, "That is all very well for you up that tree. What you don't know is that there is a bear in this cave."

How true to life that story is. How often we get upset with people who don't seem to be concentrating or listening, or who are moody or impatient. Often our impatience stems from knowing little or nothing of the bear in their cave, perhaps a deep concern for the health of a loved one, or their own health, or the behaviour of a rebellious teenage daughter, or mortgage payments, or some other problem.

How wise Robert Burns' advice was:

> *Then gently scan your brother man,*
> *Still gentler sister woman;*
> *Tho' they may gang a kennin wrang,*
> *To step aside is human.*
> *One point must still be greatly dark,*
> *The moving, Why they do it.*

Better Off Than We Imagine

A middle-aged farmer, who had lived on the same farm for twenty years, became more and more critical of it. He finally decided to sell it and buy one more to his liking. His lawyer, before sending the farmer's advertisement to the local newspaper, read it to him. Among other things it described the farm's many advantages, its ideal location, its fertile ground, modern farmhouse and kindly neighbours. After hearing the advert read a second time, the farmer said, "Look, I have changed my mind. All my life I have been looking for a farm just like that."

An architect once told me of the difficulties involved in designing the dream house. If you concentrate on designing a magnificent exterior, it will have shortcomings inside. If on the other hand you concentrate on designing the perfect interior it will very likely lose some of its exterior attraction. Just as there is no perfect farm or house, so there is no perfect school or church, village or climate. If we look for faults we will easily find them. Weeds grow in every garden. Though there are shortcomings in every teacher and minister, faults in every friend, drawbacks about every job, disadvantages in every climate, there is often, if we stop and think about it, a credit side as well.

After expressing appreciation for the bare necessities which he had on the desert island, Robinson Crusoe wrote in his diary, "All our discontents about what we want, appeared to me to spring from the want of thankfulness for what we have." It is so easy to magnify disadvantages, and forget the advantages.

The capacity to criticise must go hand in hand with the capacity to appreciate what is good and lovely. Recall the children in Maeterlinck's *Bluebird of Happiness*. They went seeking happiness in the past and the future. They returned to find it singing on their front doorstep!

What Is Love?

Love may be a universal language, but it sounds and looks different to different people. A group of professional people asked a group of 6 to 8 year olds what love is. The answers they got were more profound than they expected.

When someone loves you, the way they say your name is different.

Love is when somebody gives you some of their French fries.

Love is what makes you smile when you are tired.

If you want to learn love, you should start with someone you don't like.

Love is when Mummy gives Daddy the best piece of chicken.

Love is when a little old woman and a little old man are still best friends even after knowing each other for years.

Love is when your puppy licks your face even after you have left him alone all day.

In *Alice in Wonderland*, Humpty Dumpty says to Alice in a regal manner, "A word means what I want it to mean."

Love is such a word. It has an enormous range of meanings. It is used to describe anything from the love of money or power, to loving ice-cream or the warm feeling we have for an activity, or other people. Parental love is vitally important for the healthy development of children.

❧

Adolescent love has an enormous range of emotions, some so strong as to override reason. Young lovers, obsessed with the one they love, ascribe to him or her every virtue and merit. Merely to glimpse the one they love is to feast the soul. Those observing this phenomenon often speak of the lover's madness, or blindness. Fortunately this transient madness is often gradually transformed into enduring sanity, but not always. A point is sometimes reached when the lover's eyes are opened and he or she falls out of love as they once fell in.

❧

In his book *Edifying Discourses,* the Danish philosopher Søren Kierkegaard has a moving passage in which he seeks to answer questions about the nature of true and lasting love.

He asks what it is that makes a person great, admired by his fellows, acceptable in the sight of God?

What it is that is older than everything else?

What it is that lasts when all else disappoints?

What it is that remains when all else changes?

What it is that gives a blessing on the abundance of the gift?

What it is that changes the widow's mite into plenty?

What it is that turns the words of a simple person into wisdom?

What is it that never changes when all else changes.

To each of these questions he answers, "It is love."

Vest Sleeves

When a Quaker was told by a friend that he felt deeply for the world's needy, the Quaker asked, "Where do you feel? Do you feel in your pocket?"

Dr Ernest Campbell once entitled an address he gave, "Giving away the sleeves of your vest." The whole point of the address was that vests do not have sleeves, so giving away the sleeves of our vest amounts to giving up something up that costs us nothing. Caring love on the other hand gives generously, not counting the cost.

One of my favourite stories concerns the massive book sale for Christian Aid which St Andrew's and St George's Church in Edinburgh hold every year, a sale which annually raises well over £100,000. One year an elderly lady in the congregation handed in a bound volume of classic cartoons from early *Vanity Fair* magazines. Lady Davidson, who was in charge of the sale, realising that the book might be of considerable worth, got it professionally valued. When the minister, Dr Andrew McLellan, was informed that the volume was worth over £5,000, he thought in fairness he ought to inform Barbara of its worth, for she was not well off. He thought she might say, "You keep a thousand for Christian Aid and I will keep the rest." But when over a cup of tea Andrew told her the value of the book she had donated, her face lit up. Without hesitation, she said, "Oh I am so pleased. I never thought I would be able to give that much to Christian Aid."

Caring love not only quickens the insight, it reveals many of the deep secrets of life – that it is more blessed to give than to receive, that loving people is far more enriching than loving things, that though faith and hope are important, love is even more important. Loving other people, and being loved by others, is to feel the sun from both sides.

Doing it for Love

On a Hebridean island there lived a beautiful young woman, gentle of speech, graceful of form and bearing, and so elegant in spirit and splendid of mind, that it was widely thought she would marry a millionaire or a celebrity. But instead she married a shy islander, a man quiet of speech who dearly loved her and the companionship of the nearby hills. To those who wondered at her choice of husband, she only once gave a hint. "I sold my dreams for love, and found caring love better than all my dreams."

On Christmas Eve, a Mrs Ballenger who lived in South Carolina was busy wrapping Christmas presents. She asked her young son Richard if he would polish her shoes. With the proud smile that only an 8-year-old can muster, he later presented her shoes for inspection. His mother was so pleased with them that she gave him a dollar. On Christmas morning as she made to put on her shoes to go to church, she noticed a lump in one shoe. Taking it off she found the dollar she had given him wrapped in paper. Written in scrawly handwriting were the words, "I done it for love."

The people who steady our country are those who do things for love. For the most part they are largely unknown; most of them will never be known ... a teacher somewhere who managed to speak a word that touched off something in a pupil's mind or heart; a parent somewhere who tended the green plant of childhood and gave it strength; a woman who out of love and concern for a neighbour in need, went the second and third mile in caring ... Just as the fragrance of a flower often lingers long after it

36

has left our hands, that is true also of a kindly life lived for others.

Our chief duty is to do little tasks for others out of love, for I believe that in the great scheme of things, nothing is more important than small unremembered acts of kindness and love.

Warm Hugs

In a Kansas City church just before Christmas, Chris sat in a wheelchair at the end of a line of fourteen people who were about to become church members by profession of faith.

Chris, who suffers from seizures and developmental problems, functions like a five-year-old. His speech is sometimes hard to understand. Mobility issues confine him to a wheelchair. Some people might be tempted to ask what can Chris, by becoming a member, possibly contribute to a congregation. They assume that only people with certain physical or mental capacities have anything to offer congregational life, or absorb anything worthwhile from being part of a worshipping congregation. How mistaken they are.

Bill Timaeus, a leading office-bearer in that Kansas City congregation, writes, "Chris, more than anyone I know, embodies love. It is not sentimentality on my part to call him love incarnate. Part of the reason is that he sees other people as being in need of love and hugs, not as competitors for life's resources, or people's attention.

Bill continues: "If people want to see what love looks like, they should look at Chris as he reaches out to hug others, and overhear him saying to the minister, as he often does, 'You are so handsome today,' or saying to females who engage him in conversation, 'You are so pretty.' Chris loves to go to church and put his envelope with a couple of dollars into the offering plate. He especially loves handing out Orders of Service at Christmas to people entering the church door, and wishing them a Merry Christmas. Many enjoy his smile and his hug. Every day during his lunch break at a special care workshop, he helps a special friend by opening her plastic lunch container and placing her spoon within her reach."

Both the Kansas City congregation and the workshop Chris attends have found that they have gained greatly by the gifts and the love Chris brings.

Zero Love

A young American lady who had taken a real fancy to a man she had met and dated twice, was thrilled when one perfect Saturday morning she received a phone call from him, telling her that he had something special in mind. He would pick her up in his vintage car and they would go for a drive and a picnic. On the journey the young man seemed preoccupied. After a few lengthy silences, he told her that an event of great significance in his life was coming up. He then drove her into and around Central Park. Half way round the Park the second time, he told her that the great moment was now almost here, a moment he wanted to share with her. He was sure she would feel the same sense of excitement as himself. Slowing down he drove into a shady recess. At that carefully timed juncture the car had reached the 100,000-mile mark. The figures on the speedometer were turning slowly over as the car came to a halt.

"Everything is back to zero," said the young man with great excitement.

Later as she related the story of their day's outing to some girl friends, she said with a laugh, but also a little sadly, "Everything in our relationship is now also back to zero!"

Feeling Sorry for Oneself

Because of Victor Hugo's strong republican views, and his criticism of Napoleon III, he was exiled from his beloved France. After spending three years in Jersey, he spent the next 15 years in Guernsey. It was in the Channel Islands that he wrote many of his finest books, including *Les Miserables* and *The Hunchback of Notre Dame*. During his stay in Jersey, most evenings, he would climb the hill above the harbour. There he would sit for a little, quietly meditating. Before leaving, he would rise, select a pebble and cast it into the water beneath. One evening a little girl who was playing nearby, asked him why he came there each night to throw stones into the water. Hugo smiled and said, "Not stones, my child. I am throwing self-pity into the sea."

In that symbolic act there is a powerful lesson. Despite our many advantages, many of us have an inordinate capacity for being sorry for ourselves, for imagining that our personal pains and problems constitute the centre of the universe. It is very easy to become a grievance collector, constantly recalling occasions when we were wronged, snubbed, misunderstood or unappreciated. We go about with a lofty, frozen air of hurt, which with the passing weeks keeps getting ever loftier and frostier.

When we next find ourselves in danger of succumbing to self-pity, let us remember Victor Hugo exiled from the land he loved, and his evening ritual upon that Jersey cliff. Instead of putting our sorrows and grievances into a glass case to gloat over, or allowing them to breed like poisonous bacteria in our emotional bloodstream, imagine them to be a stone and fling them far from us with all the strength we possess. Without them we will travel with a lighter heart and surer foot.

The Unknown Future

Part of the thrill of touring in the Scottish Highlands is that the road keeps winding and disappearing. What lies ahead at the next corner is concealed until you round it. You have to wait and see what new glimpses you are going to get of the mountains and lochs. Motorways may get you there quicker, but they are nothing like as interesting or attractive as winding Highland roads on a lovely summer or autumn day. I have never forgotten the monotony of driving across the flat plains of Wyoming and Kansas, and seeing the road stretch endlessly ahead, mile after mile, hour after hour.

Many in the ancient world, craving information about future happenings, consulted the oracles of Apollo and Zeus. The prophecies they received were often worded ambiguously so as to cover all contingencies. It is little different today.

Instead of focussing on the wonder of the present and appreciating what is happening all around them, many avidly read astrological columns, longing for predictions about what lies ahead of them in the future.

I have difficulty understanding such longings, for it is the unknown character of the future that keeps my mind and heart eager and expectant. To receive bad news about what lay ahead for me or my family, would take much of the joy out of the present. Part of the thrill of reading an enthralling novel lies in not knowing the final outcome. We spoil a book when half-way through we look to the end. Watching a recording of a sports match is nothing like as enjoyable if we know the final result. For my wife, part of the charm of a few days in a hotel stems from her not knowing beforehand what she is going to have at meal-times.

I believe Al Capp was right when he said, "The man who invents a futuroid camera will have done more to make life unliveable than the man who invented the hydrogen bomb."

Precious Rubbish

When Lord Nelson was buried in St Paul's Cathedral, his coffin was carried by a detachment of sailors who had served on Nelson's ship, HMS *Victory*. Just before the sailors lowered the coffin into the crypt, the choir sang a chorus by Handel with the moving words, "His body is buried in peace, but his name liveth for evermore." After laying the Admiral's body to rest, instead of folding up the badly shot-torn flags from Nelson's ship, flags which had been used to cover his coffin as it lay in state, the sailors seized one of the flags and tore it into several pieces. They apparently had been given permission to do this. Each sailor kept a piece as a memento. Though it was only a little bit of faded coloured cloth, to these sailors it meant much more than that. It was a reminder of what Nelson had meant to them, and what he had done for their country.

I suspect that in some of our homes there is a drawer filled with what other people might well call rubbish, things we cannot bear to throw out for the simple reason that everything in that drawer reminds us of some person or some special occasion. When we take these often financially worthless things into our hands, a person or a presence or a fond memory is recalled. The drawer's contents have a value far beyond their material worth.

Interruptions

As a young minister, I used to get frustrated by interruptions. I would be working in the study on some article or sermon which I thought was extremely important. Suddenly the door or phone bell would ring. Sometimes it was a young couple to arrange a wedding, or a young lad wanting a character reference, or a passport form signed, or a daughter whose elderly father had died, or a mother of teenagers wondering if she could cope. Whatever the nature of the interruption, by the time I returned to the study, my train of thought was broken. Just as I was beginning to pick it up again, the phone or door bell would ring again. It took me several years to realise that these interruptions were in fact my work – making time to listen to those at their wits' end, making time to share the happiness of the parents of a new baby, making time to welcome the visitor and the stranger.

One of my most distinguished teachers, Professor Reinhold Neibuhr told how as a young minister, he overworked until he had a serious breakdown. He said he ought to have seen the warning signs, the clearest of which was when his students started apologising for bothering him.

The next time we are exasperated by interruptions, let us remember that their frequency may be an indicator of the contribution we are making to our common life. Only those who have the capacity to help are interrupted. One of the most awful things that could happen would be to become so independent, so unhelpful, so unneighbourly that nobody would ever interrupt us, that we would be left comfortably alone. A ringing phone can be a nuisance when you are trying to think long thoughts, but if it stopped ringing, our lives would be the poorer

For Valour

During the Crimean War, Charles Lucas was on board HMS *Hecla* when a Russian shell, its fuse hissing, landed on the ship. All the crew, except Charles, flung themselves down on the deck. With great presence of mind, Charles ran forward, picked up the shell and flung it into the sea, where it exploded with a tremendous roar before hitting the water. When Queen Victoria learned what he had done, she initiated a new award for outstanding gallantry, the Victoria Cross. Since then a number of super-heroes in the British Army, Navy and Air Force have been recipients. Bill Reid from Crieff in Perthshire was one of them. He received this award for incredible bravery during a bombing raid over Germany during the 2nd World War. He was captain of a Lancaster which took part in a raid on Dusseldorf. While passing over the Dutch coast they were attacked by a Messerschmitt. Bill's windscreen was shattered and he was wounded in the head and shoulders. Assuring his crew he was all right, he ignored the blood flowing from his injuries. As they approached Dusseldorf they were attacked by a Focke-Wulf, which raked their plane with machine-gun fire, killing the navigator and wireless operator, and putting the aircraft's oxygen and communications systems out of action. Sustained by bottled oxygen administered by his flight engineer, Bill pressed on to his target. Having released their bombs, he set off home, steering by the moon and stars.

On the day of his funeral, many years later, as the mourners left the service, the Red Arrows flew low over the church, before symbolically turning sharply upwards and disappearing into the heavens. It was a moving and unforgettable sight, a wonderful tribute to a very brave man.

This highest award for bravery is surprisingly not made of gold or silver. The original Victoria Crosses were made from metal from an old Russian gun captured during the Crimean War. On the front of the medal are carved laurel wreaths, a lion, a crown and the words 'Pro Valore' – for valour. On the back is the name of the person winning the award and the date of their act of bravery. The value of the metal and the ribbon is no more than a few pounds, and yet to the recipients' families, it is a priceless treasure, a symbol of the selfless concern for others which inspired their loved one to make an immense personal sacrifice.

War Memorials

The numerous war memorials scattered throughout our land are powerful reminders of the countless sailors, soldiers and airmen who were killed in the prime of their lives, defending our shores and our precious freedoms. I often shudder to think what would have happened to us as a nation, had Hitler's forces not been pushed back in 1940 by the brave airmen who fought in the Battle of Britain, and four years later by those who took part in the D-Day invasion.

War memorials are, however, much more than just reminders of our immense debt to the members of our armed forces who fought and died in some foreign field. They are also reminders of the pain and suffering experienced by their families and loved ones at home.

During a visit to Gallipoli, where thousands of Allied, Australian, New Zealand and Turkish soldiers were killed in the 1st World War, I was deeply moved on seeing at the entrance to a cemetery, a sculpture depicting a little girl holding in one hand some flowers, and clasping with her other hand, the wrinkled hand of an elderly gentleman walking with a stick. The girl clearly represented the daughter of a dead soldier, the man, the soldier's grandfather.

A few years ago a friend brought me from Australia a picture of a war memorial in Sydney which depicts three women standing shoulder to shoulder. They are holding aloft the body of a dead soldier. The first woman is clearly the soldier's mother, the second his wife and the third his daughter.

No heart specialist is able to cure the heartbreak of those who in time of war lose a spouse, son, father, grand-daughter or grandson. Many never really get over such a loss.

Graduation Addresses

During a Moderatorial visit to Atlanta in 1995, I was privileged to meet Tom Cousins, whose firm Cousins Enterprises built many of Atlanta's outstanding buildings. Tom is not only a committed church member but one of America's great philanthropists. Since our first meeting, we have spent a good deal of time together in America and Scotland, both on and off the golf course including the world-famous Augusta National where the Masters is played each year, and where Tom is a member. One night I shared with Tom the substance of an article I had read about professors who were asked if they could remember who the guest speaker was when they graduated. One of them laughed and said, "That is not a fair question. That was far too long ago!" Another replied, "I can remember both events, but not anything that was said."

Tom told me how he once spoke at the graduation ceremony of his old high school. He began by telling the students that he personally had no recollection who had spoken at any of his graduations. Hoping that would not be true in their case, he told them he had decided to give them each one share in his company! (A considerable gift!) "Each year when you receive the financial report you will remember who spoke to you on this significant occasion in your life!"

Like the University professors and Tom Cousins, I also cannot remember any of the guest speakers when I graduated, but I do remember reading of a graduation ceremony at McGill University in Canada where the guest speaker was Rudyard Kipling. Aware that the graduating students were living in a society that valued success, wealth and not getting caught, he warned them against becoming too obsessed with the big pay cheque, or the next promotion or the larger house. He then added, "Some day you will meet a truly good person who is not obsessed with any of these things, and then you will know how poor you really are."

Perfect Means, Confused Ends

Malcolm Muggeridge, the former editor of *Punch* magazine, confessed in his later years that what bothered him most was not any sin of commission or omission to be repented of, but that he had chosen the third-rate over the first-rate. He had gone after the worst when he could have had the best. He had chosen processed cheese when he could have had cheddar, artificial flowers when primroses were out.

Writing of the era in which he lived, Albert Einstein said, "We live in an age of perfect means and confused ends." Confused ends was the theme of an address given by the author Anna Quindlen at the graduation ceremony of students at Villanova University in America. She told those graduating how once, when she was beginning to prosper, she received a postcard on which her father, who could be very blunt, had written, "Never forget Anna that if you win the rat race, you are still a rat." She then went on to say to the students, "Be careful not to confuse your life and your work. The second is only part of the first. You cannot be really first rate at your work if your work is all you are. Everyone wants to do well, but if you do not do good, then doing well will never be enough."

Survival of the Fittest

This phrase, "the survival of the fittest", first used to describe Darwin's theory of evolution, was coined by the distinguished biologist and philosopher Herbert Spencer. Spencer's phrase, along with a phrase of Darwin's, "the preservation of favoured races in the struggle for life", lent themselves to misinterpretation and misapplication. Both Spencer and Darwin would have been horrified to think that some industrialists and colonialists would seize on these phrases to justify the continued exploitation of men, women and children in factories and mines, and those in foreign lands whom colonialists regarded as belonging to 'inferior races'.

Spencer would also have disapproved of the conclusions which the German philosopher Nietzsche drew from the phrase, "the survival of the fittest". Believing that self-interest and the will to power were what mattered most, Nietzsche dismissed the Jewish and Christian ethic of kindness and caring for the weak, as a 'false morality'. Nietzsche's writings later exercised a profound influence on the thinking of the Nazi leaders. Convinced that the Germans were the Master Race, they advocated the sterilisation of unwanted types, and the extermination of 'inferior peoples' such as Jews, gypsies and the mentally ill. In *Mein Kampf,* Hitler wrote, "Nature only allows the most healthy to survive in the struggle for life."

Thomas Huxley, another distinguished 19th-century biologist, argued that more important than the survival of the fittest, was the fitting of as many as possible to survive, that in place of ruthless self-assertion there should be self-restraint, that instead of trampling down competitors, people should respect their fellows and cooperate with them. He wrote, "The good of mankind means the attainment by every man of all the happiness which he can enjoy, without diminishing the happiness of others."

Out of the thunder of contemporary events, all the hurt, fighting, callousness and injustice in our world, one fact seems to be emerging, the obligation of humanity to stop living by the principle of the survival of the fittest or the most powerful, and live instead by the supreme principle of caring love.

The Quest for Truth

"The God Delusion" and "The Virus of Faith" were the provocative titles of two television programmes about Professor Richard Dawkins, the militant atheist. The professor of biology at Oxford was invited by Channel 4 to share with viewers his controversial beliefs that religious faith is not just a delusion, but a pathological and highly destructive virus, spread from one generation to another. Dawkins is convinced that science has made religion untenable.

I wish that, before broadcasting his views, Professor Dawkins, instead of interviewing for his book several extreme and rather scary religious freaks, had taken the time to meet and speak with the former Chief Rabbi Jonathan Sacks, Sir John Polkinghorne, a Nobel laureate in quantum physics, Francis Collins, who directed the team responsible for the mapping of the human genome, and Rowan Williams the former Archbishop of Canterbury, all of whom worship God with their minds as well as their hearts. Had he done so, he might well have been more hesitant to say that "all bright people have had the wisdom to reject the discredited convictions of their forebears", and that "intellectuals no longer bother with religion."

Science and religion need each other. They are cousins in the quest for truth. Science is about explanation. It explores and examines the order of the physical world, a world shot through with many indications of a creative mind having been at work. Religion is about meaning. As Rabbi Sacks says, "Religion at its finest seeks to join things together so that they tell a story, and to join people together so that they form relationships. Science takes things apart to see how they work. Religion seeks to put things together in an attempt to understand what they mean." The binocular vision which science and religion provide, helps me see and understand more than I would with only one of them.

More thoughtful and respectful dialogue between science and religion could offer great benefits to society, scientists being invited to address the deep moral issues raised by their research, while religious people are challenged to articulate a more rigorous and rational faith. My own faith has certainly been enhanced by a willingness to confront the intellectual challenges of science.

Ultimate Meaning

An astrophysicist recently told those scientists, poets and philosophers who speak of meaning and purpose in the universe, to save their breath to cool their porridge, for that kind of talk is silly. In effect he was saying there is no answer to the question of ultimate meaning.

For many years Albert Camus, the French Nobel Prize winning novelist, also believed we live in a world without meaning. His early writings gave rise to the philosophy known as Absurdism. In his book *The Outsider*, the chief character has no roots, no answer to the great questions concerning life's ultimate meaning and purpose. Later in his life, however, Camus wrestled with the question, 'How do we value our life if it has no meaning?' What few of Camus' readers know is that shortly before his premature death as a result of a road accident, Camus attended the American Church in Paris. To a reporter (Howard Mouma), who questioned Camus about his change in outlook, he said, "The reason I have been coming to church is because I am seeking ... something to fill the void I am experiencing ... I am searching for something that the world is not giving me." Science and technology have been responsible for some of the greatest achievements in the human story, but they do not answer the three questions most people ask at some time in their lives, "Who am I?", "Why am I here?", "And how then shall I live?"

The American poet Robert Frost once asked a group of university students who had gathered to hear him read some of his poetry, if they thought their minds had been created mindlessly, if they thought their ability to act purposefully had been brought about simply by accident. He asked them if they believed that a rational world had an irrational origin, or if the universe, which seems more and more like a great thought, was in fact only the result of two blind children, Chance and Accident, making mud pies in the dark. Frost said he personally could not accept that. Nor can I.

The Sea in Reverse

At the end of the Second World War, Adolf Eichmann is reported to have said, "I have nothing to confess. I did nothing wrong. I have no regrets." Unlike Eichmann, as many look back on their life, they have considerable regrets. Our lives resemble the sea – in reverse! Whereas calm reigns far beneath the churning of the ocean's mighty waves, the opposite is true in many a life. Beneath apparently confident exteriors there are often troubled hearts and acute feelings of regret.

Loss of self-respect can be painful. Three o'clock in the morning has been described as 'the dark night of the soul', the hour when we lie awake acutely conscious of some thoughtless remark we made, or hating ourselves for something we did, such as sacrificing integrity for the quick buck, or seeking to prove our superiority by making another feel inferior.

A psychiatrist once asked a patient who had attempted suicide, "What part of you did you want to kill?" A good question. Most of us can think of unruly parts of our natures we would like to bury, elements in our character we long to be rid of, painful memories we would love to put to rest so that they can no longer torment us. In one of his short stories, O'Henry told of a thief who sat one evening smoking a cigar in a park. That day he had swindled a child out of a dollar bill for breakfast, and tricked an old man out of a wad of notes for dinner. He sat chuckling at the thought of his successful day. Just then a young woman dressed in white passed by, hurrying home. There was a purity and honesty about her face. Several years previously he had sat on the same bench as her at school. What a lovely girl she had been. What happy times they had had. Suddenly the thief got up, laid his burning face against a lamp-post and cried, "I wish I could die."

Buying Shoes

"Never buy shoes in the morning." That was a wise old piece of market-place advice, for in the course of the day our feet do tend to swell slightly. Shoes bought in the morning can be uncomfortable by the end of the day. Shoes ought to be fitted at the point of maximum need.

It likewise concerns me that many young people, early on in their lives, settle for an outlook on life, and goals in life that will not ultimately satisfy, that will not meet the demands of their middle and later years. Many look for thrills in the wrong places. Many voices shout at them, "This is the way. Walk ye in it." Whereas some outlooks on life enlarge and enrich life, others like "Your worth is what you can afford", or, as one controversial advert recently put it, "Life is short, have an affair", impoverish life. Not all roads lead to the peak of the same mountain – some like self-interest, lust and acquisitiveness lead over the precipice.

Emerson's words, "Whoso would be a man must be a non-conformist", are at best a half-truth. Though there can be value in questioning and re-examining accepted beliefs and ways, rebellion for the sake of rebellion has often resulted in young people, like the prodigal son, falling for the first alternative life style or cult they come across.

Suffering from a Sunset

While on holiday, a grandfather took his little grandson for a walk. On their walk they met a disgruntled elderly gentleman whom the grandfather had known many years before. That day the man's moaning and groaning were aggravated by his having had a touch of sunstroke. Shortly after continuing their walk, the grandson looked up and said, "Grandpa, I hope you never suffer from a sunset."

I am sure all of us know people who as they grow older, live in what I am tempted to call the object-ive mood. They become more critical and cynical. But I can think of others for whom advancing years has been a time of blossoming, a time of fulfilment. Though they have grown old on the outside, they have not grown old in the inside. Just as old wine bottles often contain the most delightful wine, and the more gnarled the cherry tree often the greater the profusion of blossoms, so there are compensations about growing old. The most valuable knowledge I have acquired with age, is not the knowledge of formulae or academic studies, but the knowledge of people, places visited and things done, knowledge gained by touch, sight, successes, failures, devotion, faith and love.

My hope is that I will die young in spirit and outlook as late as possible, that I will grow old without resentment or self-pity, that I will continue to use each new day well. Many a good tune has been played on an old fiddle. We are not really old if our song is not sung, our spring has not sprung and our fun is not done!

❦

I recall a 76-year-old man who objected to being called elderly. He associated the word with being incapable, joining the sunset brigade, those who are on the way out and sinking fast. He thought that as soon as anyone called him elderly, he might as well take to his bed and dribble! Although there are health problems associated with ageing – knee, hip, heart and memory problems – there is also, as a friend once said, "a lot of sugar at the bottom of the cup." Though now an octogenarian, I keep telling myself that eighty is the new sixty! Though my golf handicap keeps rising, and my drives keep getting shorter, I am fortunate that I can still enjoy, in the company of good friends, nine holes of golf. Though there is now considerably less to my future than there is to my past, retirement allows my wife and me to spend more time with family and old friends, to make new friends, to read books, watch sport and drama on television, to listen to great music, and continue to use what time and strength we have to help those whose health is poorer and whose needs are greater. The French writer Albert Camus said, "To grow old is to pass from passion to compassion." I like that.

Child-like not Childish

There is a major difference between being childish and child-like. Childishness is something we must outgrow. "When I became a man" said St Paul, "I put away childish things" – throwing tantrums, being self-centred and inconsiderate, and crying when we don't get our own way. Being child-like on the other hand is a wonderful virtue. To a young child, a person's rank or colour do not matter. The prince's son will play happily with the bricklayer's, the little white boy with the little black boy, until adult prejudice spoils the friendship. Young children do not hide their feelings. Their impulses are not strangled by prudent calculations. If they are happy they laugh or jump for joy. Only later do they begin to worry about the impression they are making. "What will people think of me?" Then they often hide their unhappiness and disguise their joy.

During one of his campaigns in the 1950s for the American Presidency, Adlai Stevenson asked some children in the audience, "How many of you would like to be President?" Many youngsters raised their hands. Adlai Stevenson then asked, "I wonder how many candidates for the presidency would like to be children again?" At that point he raised his own hand. Many secretly wish they were child-like again, that they had not lost the child's spontaneity, enthusiasm, trustfulness and sense of wonder.

Picasso's burning desire was to see the world as a child, for in the eyes of the child there are not seven wonders of the world, there are seven million! Children also have a remarkable capacity to forgive and forget remarks and incidents that in the adult world often become permanent grudges. Though children quarrel, they are often soon back playing together. Adults on the other hand tend to allow sores and verbal wounds to fester.

Remaining Child-like

Dr Albert Schweitzer, a Nobel Peace Prize winner, was one of the wisest and most compassionate people of the 20th century. By the age of thirty, he was a professor in a German university, a doctor of philosophy, a doctor of music and a doctor of theology. But then he decided to study medicine so that he could go to West Africa and try and repay a little of the debt which he believed the white man owed the black man. One day as Dr Schweitzer was working putting a new roof on the hospital at Lambaréné, he shouted over to a black man who was sitting nearby, "Could you give me a hand with this timber?" When the man, whose wife was a patient in the hospital, declined saying, "Sorry you see I am an intellectual", Dr Schweitzer, the former brilliant academic said, "I once tried to be that too, but I could not live up to it!"

I was introduced to Albert Schweitzer's story by my English teacher at school. In my 5th year, Mr Thomson suggested I read George Seaver's biography of Schweitzer. Not only did that book markedly influence my under-standing of life, it helped me pass my Higher English exam! In the morning paper, the possible essay titles about which we had to write included 'the doctor'. I chose to write about Dr Schweitzer. In the afternoon literature paper, one of the choices we were given, was to write about a biography that had made an impact on us. Again I wrote about Albert Schweitzer, hoping that it would not be the same examiner that would mark both papers!

Looking back on his life, Schweitzer told how he had tried not to become what is generally understood by the term a man of ripe experience, one who once believed in the victory of truth and goodness, who was once zealous for justice and capable of enthusiasm, but is no longer. Schweitzer believed that it is through the idealism of youth that we catch sight of truth, and in that idealism we possesses a wealth we must never exchange for anything else. He wanted people to get back in touch with the child they once were.

Just Kidding

A school bus driver tells how when she stopped the bus to pick up little Chris for nursery school, she noticed an older woman hugging him as he left the house. "Is that your grandmother?" the driver asked. "Yes," Chris said, "she has come to stay for a week." "How nice," she said. When the driver then asked the little boy where his grandmother lived, he replied, "At the train station. Whenever we need her we just go there and get her."

❧

A grandmother tells how one of the village's biggest social events was the Christmas concert at the school. Her small grandson was very excited at being involved in this great affair. School was dismissed early that eagerly awaited day, so that everyone could rest before the evening performance. When her grandson arrived home, he noticed that his teenage sister was doing her hair, and his mother was pressing his father's suit. Somewhat concerned, he asked "Where are you all going?" "To your Christmas concert dear," said his mother. "Didn't you think we were going?" "Well," he said, "I did not think you would have to come to the school. I thought you would be watching it on television."

❧

An eight-year-old boy was teaching a little girl to ride his bicycle. The little girl, who was fair and pretty, kept falling off. After one such fall she turned, and said with a laugh, "It takes real brains to be as stupid as I am!"

❧

When in a general knowledge quiz a teenage girl was asked, "What does a blindfolded woman holding a pair of scales symbolise?" she tentatively suggested, "Weight-watchers?"

❧

After tucking their 3-year-old son Sam into bed, his parents heard sobbing coming from his room. Rushing back in, they found him crying hysterically. He told them he had swallowed a penny and he was sure he was going to die. No amount of talking helped. In an attempt to calm him, his father took a penny from his pocket and pretended to pull it out of Sam's ear. Sam was delighted. Taking the penny from his father's hand he proceeded to swallow it, before cheerfully saying, "Do it again Dad."

❧

A primary school teacher asked her class to complete some well-known proverbs. There were some interesting answers.

Don't bite the hand that ... looks dirty.

A penny saved is ... not much.

Laugh and the world laughs with you; cry and ... you have to blow your nose.

When the blind lead the blind ... get out of the way.

❧

A mother tells how nervous she was the night her husband took her and their three young children to a smart restaurant for the first time. When the waiter brought the bottle of wine her Dad had ordered, he uncorked it and poured a small amount for her to taste. It was then their six-year-old piped up, "Mummy usually drinks a lot more than that."

❧

A wee lad, who had been at church with his parents, asked them as they left the church, "You know how at the end of the prayers, we say Amen. Is that like pressing the send button on the computer?"

❧

A paediatric nurse tells how one of her most difficult tasks is immunising children. One day a four-year-old, on seeing the needle, screamed at her, "No, No, No." When her mother scolded her and told her she ought to be more polite, the girl screamed even louder, "No thank you! No thank you!"

A five-year-old boy had gone with his Mum to see a young couple's new baby. Having gazed and gazed at the small, red wrinkled face, he said to his Mum as they left the ward, "I am not surprised Aunt Mary hid him for so long under her dress."

The Rev. Donald McQuarrie, formerly of Fort William, relates how the Sunday before Easter he was telling the children the Bible story about Jesus, just before his arrest, telling Peter, who was protesting his loyalty, that before the cock crowed he would deny him three times. Donald then went on to tell the children how shortly after Jesus was arrested, a maid in the palace of King Herod, to which Jesus had been taken, said to Peter, who had followed Jesus, "You were one of them." Peter denied this, saying, "I do not know the man." When the maid said a second time, "You were one of them", Peter again denied it even more vehemently. After the accusation had been made a third time, and again denied by Peter, the cock was heard to crow. Having built up to this climax, Donald then asked the children what they thought Peter did on hearing the cock crow. Whereas one wee girl suggested that he probably cried with shame, a slightly older boy said, "I think he would probably go out and ring its neck!"

For several years the Rev. David Hamilton was the minister in the village of Rannoch which lies at the foot of Schiehallon, Perthshire's best known mountain. From Rannoch, the mountain looks like a massive pyramid. David tells how during his time there, a father, mother and small boy had moved from industrial Lanarkshire with its coal mines and coal bings to Rannoch. They arrived after darkness had fallen. Early the following morning the parents were wakened by their excited six-year-old dashing into their bedroom, shouting, "Dad you should see the size of the bing outside our house!"

❧

At Bridgeton Cross in Glasgow five major roads met. Often these roads were jammed with traffic. One day the policeman on duty noticed a little girl, about ten years of age, standing on the pavement with her wee sister, who would be about five. They had a ramshackle pram with a baby in it. Stopping all the traffic he signalled to them to cross. All went fine until they were mounting the pavement at the other side. Suddenly the front wheel came off the ramshackle pram, it toppled over and out rolled the baby. Leaving the traffic to take care of itself, the white-coated policeman went over to where the pram lay. Handing the baby to the older girl, he somehow managed to get the wheel back on. The girl and the very little girl and the ramshackle pram then continued on their way, but after going about twenty yards, the procession came to a halt. The older girl said something to the younger girl. The outcome of the conversation was that they returned to where the policeman had helped them. When he went over to see if anything was wrong, the ten-year-old put her hand into her pocket, pulled out a sticky bit of toffee, and said to the policeman, "Sir, for helping us, would you like to have a suck at my toffee?" Taking off his white gloves he took a lick. Then drawing himself up to his full height he thanked and saluted her.

※

A paediatric nurse tells how one day at the clinic she handed a young patient a urine sample container and told him to go and fill it in the toilet. A few minutes later he returned with an empty container. "I did not need it," he said. "There was a W.C. in there."

※

A mother who was checking her 13-year-old's homework on antonyms (word opposites) was surprised to realise how much attention he had paid to her shopping habits. Opposite the word 'bought', he had printed as its opposite 'returned'.

※

When a mother asked her four year old daughter who had gone fishing with her father, if they had caught anything, she replied, "No we just drowned some maggots."

※

An infant teacher asked her class to draw something beginning with the letter T. One little boy decided to draw "tights". When he had finished, the teacher asked him why he had only drawn a rectangle, the wee lad said, "They are still in the packet."

※

A father out driving with his six-year-old son passed a greyhound track. Not having seen one before, the boy asked what it was. When told that it was a place where people go to race dogs, his son said, "I bet the dogs win."

❧

A grandmother tells how she was standing in the kitchen chatting to her tall slim daughter, when her grandson came into the room. "Grandma," he said, "Mummy is much taller than you." "Yes she is," said his grandmother with mock sadness. "But don't worry, Grandma," he continued after a sympathetic pause, "you are much wider."

❧

A teacher who had asked her class to write about their homes, tells how one girl wrote that in their lounge there was a "3p suite".

❧

A mother tells how when her little girl came home from school and announced, "I kissed a boy today, Mummy," she swallowed hard at the prospect of pre-teen dating, before asking, "How did you manage that?" "Some of the other girls helped hold him down."

❧

When a young lad saw a poster advertising a mathematics conference, the theme of which was "A Way with Maths", he turned to his Mum and said hopefully, "Do you think they will really do away with maths?"

❧

When some new people moved into their street, the six-year-old daughter of a neighbour knocked on their door and introduced herself: "Hello, my name is Joanne. Do you have any children I could play with?" When the lady of the house explained that her children were all grown up, Joanne said, "Oh never mind, I should have called earlier."

❧

A wife tells how during her husband's time as a mature student, they did not have much money. At a friend's wedding, her youngest daughter was sitting next to her when the minister asked the bridal couple, "Do you take this man for better or worse, for richer or poorer, in sickness and in health?" her daughter turned to her and whispered loudly, "You chose poorer, didn't you Mummy?"

❧

When a nurse at the surgery asked a patient if she had a name for the baby she was expecting, she replied. If it is a girl we shall call her Elizabeth." Then looking at her four small sons, she added ruefully, "If it is another boy we shall call it a day."

❧

Children's parties remind you there are children worse than yours.

❧

How technology has changed things, even children's games. A Glaswegian who was passing a group of children playing hide and seek, heard one of the lads saying to another, "It is your turn to hide. Phone us when you are ready."

Fear – A Blessing or a Curse?

During the 2nd World War a radio commentator, when announcing the number of German planes that had been shot down, fell into the habit of ending each announcement with the exclamation, "Who is afraid of the Focke-Wulf?" (Focke-Wulf being a type of fighter plane and the nickname for the German air force.) An RAF pilot finally sent the radio announcer a picture of his crew. On the back he had written, "Who is afraid of the Focke-Wulf? We are." The entire crew had signed their names. A courageous person is not one who has no fear, but one who is prepared to act bravely. In *Moby Dick*, the captain said he would have no man on his boat who did not fear whales.

Too many articles in magazines on how to get rid of fear are unsatisfying. They start from the premise that fear is an enemy, a harmful emotion to be driven out. Now there is no doubt that when fear overleaps its proper boundaries, when it becomes abnormal and irrational, it can become a destructive, disintegrating force. Countless phobias are listed in the dictionary, from claustrophia, the fear of being shut in, to phobophobia, the fear of fear. Such phobias are not only very real but can be crippling psychologically.

But fear itself is an elemental emotion with a constructive, emotional purpose. For creatures like the deer and the rabbit, fear is a major weapon of defence. The sense of impending danger starts a nervous reaction which shoots a powerful stimulant into their glands, resulting in them travelling faster than they otherwise would. When Pauline Cafferkey, the brave Lanarkshire nurse, first volunteered to go out to Sierra Leone to care for Ebola sufferers, she was asked if she wasn't afraid of catching the dread disease. She frankly admitted she was afraid, but hoped that very fear would intensify the precautions she and the other volunteers would take.

Wise parents teach their children to have healthy fears, such as playing with electricity and fire, or rusty razorblades, or swimming in deep quarries, or dabbling in drugs. They know that such fears can often be the starting point of wisdom.

Solitude and Loneliness

The naturalist Henry Thoreau said that although he did not have a drawing room in his little cabin in the woods, he had a 'withdrawing room'! From times of 'withdrawal', he received refreshment of mind and spirit. Quiet times, when we reflect for a little on what it means to be fully human, can be as beneficial for mental and spiritual health, as vitamins and exercise are for physical health.

Periods of reflection can make us more relevant doers. Picasso said, "Without great solitude, no serious work is possible." Mozart would have agreed: "When I am entirely alone and of good cheer – say travelling in a carriage or walking after a good meal, or during the night when I cannot sleep – it is on such occasions that my ideas flow best and most abundantly."

Solitude, making time to be alone, is however a very different thing from the painful loneliness which too many people experience . Whereas solitude expresses the glory of being alone, loneliness expresses its pain. Long ago the Psalmist cried, "Hear my cry O God. From the end of the earth I cry to you." His phrase 'the end of the earth' describes that place where one feels utterly lonely. Its location is spiritual, not geographical. The phrase has far more affinity with being at our wit's end, than Land's End.

Nothing crushes the human spirit more than loneliness. The painful sense of isolation robs people of everything but time. It is as harmful to people's health as smoking and obesity. Solitary confinement is such an awful form of punishment, that it is now seldom used. Yet outside our prisons many elderly folk are effectively living in solitary confinement, alone not just one day, but every day. Terry Waite told how one of the few positive things about his four years as a hostage in Lebanon, chained to a radiator, was that it gave him a deeper understanding of those who are hostages as a result of ill-health, those confined for months and sometimes years to the same four walls.

Dreaming Dreams

The playwright Bernard Shaw wrote, "You see things that are, and say why. I dream of things that might be and say why not?" What a debt we owe people who not only dreamt dreams, but by hard work and considerable sacrifice, succeeded in giving substance to their dreams. What a debt we also owe to those who, realising that some cherished dream would never come to pass, settled down and served faithfully in some less exciting sphere.

Biography is full of shattered dreams and disappointments. David Livingstone wanted to go as a missionary to China, but on learning that was not possible, went to Africa instead. Walter Scott wanted to excel in poetry, but realising he could never match Byron, took to writing novels. Few live their lives on the basis of their first choice. For many, a physical handicap, or lack of academic qualifications or some unexpected family circumstance, made impossible a career they longed to follow. For others the dream of spending many happy years with their spouse has been shattered by a serious accident or illness. Running through many a life is a river of grief and disappointment.

For some people, such setbacks silence the music of living. They indulge in that subtle but dangerous luxury of self-pity. Thankfully others, instead of sitting down and crying over spilt milk, rise up and act. They make the best of what, at the time, they were sure was second best. Disappointment for them is not a terminus. When St Paul was not allowed to go to Bithynia, he immediately wondered if there was someone whose life might be changed and enriched because he had landed in Troas. And of course there was.

Just as the best cook is the one who on a Friday makes a fine meal out of the week's left-overs, so in life some of the finest banquets that have been spread for the enrichment of humanity, have been made out of the left-overs of disappointed hopes and shattered dreams. Far more important than what happens to people is their reaction to what happens to them.

Let There Be Light

In the chancel of Dornoch Cathedral there are three stained glass windows in memory of Andrew Carnegie, the American steel baron and generous philanthropist. The windows remind us of three of the causes he supported, causes very dear to his heart – libraries, music and world peace.

In the library window, which depicts a lady holding a book, there are the words "Let there be light", words which Carnegie had inscribed on the outside of all the 3,000 free libraries he gifted. The Dornoch Library is an exception, in that there the words are carved in Gaelic not English.

Carnegie's boast that "the sun never set on a Carnegie Free Library" was probably justified. Dornoch, Edinburgh, Pittsburgh, Dallas and Dunedin and hundreds of other towns and cities were the recipients of one of his libraries. The arrangement was that he would provide the building, but the local people had to provide the books.

A second window depicts an organ and many other musical instruments. It is a reminder of Carnegie's many gifts to the world of music. He helped found the Pittsburgh Philharmonic orchestra, and finance the New York Philharmonic. Having built the Carnegie Concert Hall in Manhattan, he invited Tchaikovsky to come for the grand opening ceremony and conduct several of his own compositions.

The third window depicts Carnegie's deep concern for world peace. He had an implacable hatred of war. "War," he said, "decides not in favour of the nation which is right, but always in favour of that which is strong." He would have warmly responded to a toast which was once proposed to weapons of war: "May they rust in peace." He would also have agreed with Martin Luther King who said, "Wars are poor chisels for carving out peaceful tomorrows ..."

In countless ways Carnegie tried to prevent the outbreak of the 1st World War. To promote peace, he built the magnificent Peace Palace in the Hague. To win President Roosevelt over to his crusade, he paid for him to have a lengthy safari in Africa. It broke Carnegie's heart when in 1914 war was declared. When he died in 1919 someone wrote,

Beyond the dark Brook of the Shadow he's gone
On over the hills and the moors toward the dawn
This Laird o' the castle by Dornoch's grey Firth
To find the Great Peace he had sought for on earth.

The Reward of Work

In his book entitled *The Road to Character*, David Brooks, the distinguished American journalist and political commentator, makes the important distinction between what he calls résumé virtues and eulogy virtues. Résumé virtues, what we call CVs, are those degrees and skills that we bring to the workplace and marketplace, and the successes achieved through competition with others. Eulogy virtues on the other hand, are those that one day might hopefully be highlighted at our funeral or in our obituary – virtues such as kindness, humility, courage, generosity, honesty and compassion.

When the father of a student in his late twenties, who had been at university for many years, studying for one degree after another, was asked what his son was going to be when he left university, the father replied, "An old man!" Though a humorous reply, the question, "What will your son be when he leaves university?" is, I believe, a more important question than the one many young people are asked – "What are you going to do when you leave school or university?"

"The primary reward for human toil," said John Ruskin the British philosopher, "is not what you earn from it, but what you become by it." Ruskin knew that life's true riches are to be found, not in the material things we live with, but in what we live for; not in salaries and status, but in human relationships. Now there is nothing wrong with a large pay-packet, but when life tumbles in, when we are depressed or lonely, when a close friend dies, or we receive a medical diagnosis we feared, it is not to our bank account or material possessions we turn for comfort and support, it is to people who love us, people we can phone or meet for a coffee or lunch, friends willing to listen.

Friends or Enemies

In one of the Harry Potter books, Neville Longbottom takes a stand against his friends Ron, Hermione and Harry because he believes that what they are doing is wrong. He appeals to a higher standard than loyalty to friends, and is willing to act on this. Towards the end of the book, the headmaster of Hogwarts school when talking about Neville, reminds the assembled students that though it takes great courage to stand up to our enemies, we need even more to stand up to our friends. The headmaster knew it is more difficult to take a different stance from friends and colleagues, than from one's enemies.

Some years ago an interesting experiment was carried out by a psychologist in Manchester. Nine young people were taken into his confidence. He told them he was going to invite eight other young people to join them, one by one. The simple experiment involved counting the beats of a metronome. He wanted each of them to add one to the number of beats he played. The tenth person was to know nothing of this prior arrangement.

Stopping the metronome after ten beats, he then asked the nine how many beats they had counted. All said eleven. With one exception the people who joined them one by one, also said 11. The psychologist later tried a similar experiment with maths students. The original nine were asked to give the same wrong answer to a not too difficult maths problem. Again the tenth person almost always gave the same wrong answer. When asked later why they gave the answer they did, they said that although they felt it was the wrong answer, they did not want to look stupid in the eyes of the others. The point of the experiment was to show that the majority of people do not like to be different from, or stand out from the crowd. The experiment confirmed that friends can sometimes be our worst enemies. How many young people have started smoking and taking drugs because they did not want to be different from their friends.

Gossip

Gossip, which is as universal as eating and sleeping, is not always malicious or negative. A kindly wee blether can be therapeutic. It can enable us to share our joys and anxieties. It can strengthen community bonds. It can also shed light on how other people cope with the worst that happens to them. In the days before radio communication, the Danish explorer Ejnar Mikkelsen was stranded for two years in the Arctic with only a few fellow explorers. He spoke later of how the silence had been as awful as the intense cold and the shortage of provisions. "Our only relief was gossip."

The word gossip came from two Anglo-Saxon words, 'god-sib', 'sib' being related to the word sibling. A gossip originally played a kindly supportive role. Queen Elizabeth accepted the office of 'gossip' at the baptism of James VI of Scotland. Unfortunately the word now tends to be associated with people who dine out on other people's shortcomings and mistakes. Too often a gossip is the enemy rather than the promoter of goodwill.

Unkind gossip is the misuse of a good attribute. It stems from an interest in others which has been corrupted. Many gossip to feed their sense of superiority, to bolster their social egos, to garnish their own traits by tarnishing other people's. Other people's faults are like the headlights in a car. They always seem more glaring than our own. The failings of colleagues for which we have the quickest eye, often shed light on our own failings. It takes a thief to catch a thief.

Harmful Rumours

Within a few weeks of a lovely widow moving into a village with her three children, she was the most talked about woman in the place. She was too pretty. Several men had been seen visiting her. Her children roamed the streets. She was lazy and spent most of her time lying on the sofa reading. One morning when she collapsed in the post office, the truth came out. She was suffering from a terminal illness. She had not the strength to do her housework. She sent her children out when the drugs could not control her pain. "I wanted them to think of me as always happy," she said. The men visitors were her family doctor, her lawyer and her husband's brother.

I often think the commandment which is most broken is "You shall not bear false witness against your neighbour." On the walls of his dining room Saint Augustine inscribed the words, "He who speaks an evil word about an absent person is not welcome at this table." An alternative punishment might be for spreaders of unkind gossip to have to listen to the gossip circulating about themselves!

Dr Allport made four helpful suggestions about how to control the flow of harmful rumours.

• Don't be afraid to ask for evidence to support the rumour. If it is not forthcoming let the rumour stop with you

• Ask yourself concerning those passing on the unkind story, "Do they have a feeling of jealousy, personal hostility or prejudice against the subject of the gossip?"

• Ask whether the gossip you are about to relate, reveals any of your own psychic dirty linen.

• Face up to your own weaknesses, or as Jesus put it, "Do something about the beam in your own eye, before you seek to remove the mote in another's eye."

One more suggestion. Practise the art of good gossip. Develop the habit of looking for the good in others, and comment on that.

An All Too Common Jail

A wealthy man once asked a bachelor friend, "Why do people criticise me for being miserly? Everyone knows I will leave everything to charity when I die." "Well," said the friend, "let me tell you about a pig and a cow. The pig was lamenting to the cow one day, how unpopular he was. 'People,' he said, 'are always talking to me about your gentleness and your kind eyes. Now admittedly you give milk and cream, but I give more. I give bacon and ham. They even pickle my feet! But still nobody likes me. Why is this?' The cow thought for a minute before saying, 'Well, maybe it is because I give while I am still living.'"

Too many people imprison themselves in a little cell of personal advantage. This often leads them in unfortunate directions. They succumb to the temptation to use other people as a means of getting things for themselves. They see themselves as superior to everyone else. They crave for constant recognition. They retreat from involvement in causes bigger than themselves. The final result is often a hardness of heart.

On the other hand going the second mile, sharing and caring, giving and forgiving. showing tender mercy to those weary from travelling while we are still alive, enlarges and enriches life. Shakespeare's Mark Antony was wrong when he said that "the evil that men do lives after them, the good is oft interred with their bones". The good we do does live after us. It is probably the most important thing we leave behind. The philosopher Descartes said, "I think therefore I am." I believe he would have been nearer the truth, had he said, "I care therefore I am." We warm to people who share from their heart and not from their ego.

More important than making something of ourselves, is finding something worth doing, and losing ourselves in it. "No tree," said Martin Luther, "bears fruit for its own self."

Clever or Wise

It is one thing to be clever and well-informed. It is another to be wise, to have discernment and right judgment. Many books read, innumerable facts memorised, do not necessarily constitute wisdom. A person can be a walking encylopedia, and have a string of university degrees, and yet speak and act like a fool. My father was never near a university, yet he was wise, in that he was skilled in the art of living. He had emotional intelligence. It was not the things he bought that shaped our lives. It was the wisdom, faith, and values that he shared with us.

Whereas in the 16th century Scotland had four universities, England only had two, Oxford and Cambridge. Scottish universities in these early days not only sought to train people for a career or a profession, they also had a deep concern to provide students with an understanding of the meaning and purpose of life. Modern universities continue to train people for the career of their choice. The benefits of this are immense. The resultant scientific, medical and technological advances have brought many blessings in their train. But some of the other early concerns of our universities have unfortunately been lost. Education has certainly become more utilitarian, more and more geared to preparing students for a life of earning.

This was a concern of Aldous Huxley. He wrote, "Many who are able to stay the course of an academic education emerge from the ordeal either as parrots, gabbling remembered formulæ ... or as specialists, knowing everything about one subject, and taking no interest in anything else, or finally as intellectuals, theoretically knowledgeable about everything, but hopelessly inept in the affairs of ordinary life. They have no integrating principle in terms of which they can arrange and give significance to such knowledge as they may subsequently acquire." Though Huxley was at times guilty of overstatement, the dangers he highlighted about the vacuum at the centre of the educational process, are real.

The Wise Club

In 1995 I was invited to preach at the Special Service of Thanksgiving to commemorate the 500th anniversary of the founding of Aberdeen University. By way of preparation I read a newly published history of the University. One chapter especially interested me. It told how in the 18th century, professors and lecturers from various faculties regularly met together in a club significantly called "The Wise Club". The titles of the subjects they discussed make fascinating reading. One lecture was on 'Taste', another on 'Genius', another on the 'Nature of Truth', and another on 'The Principles of Common Sense'. They knew that interests outwith their own specialised field helped make them more rounded personalities. It is not healthy for a teacher only to be able to talk about teaching, or a minister only about the church, or a doctor to have no other interests but medicine.

In the final year of my science studies, one of my lecturers, a Dr Burton, told us how that summer he had attended an international conference on nuclear physics. He said it was so specialised that the only paper he really understood was the one he delivered himself! The same is often true of other science and medical conferences. In the setting of a modern university it is very easy to lose the wider and more inclusive understanding of knowledge.

One aspect of the genius and steadiness of our Scottish forebears, an aspect that contributed to many of them being, as Robert Burns said, 'loved at home, revered abroad', stemmed from the fact that from an early age they were brought up to ponder life's big questions such as

"What is man's chief end?" The understanding that life is a sacred trust, given to us to enrich the life of the great human family, that is still the beginning of wisdom. The neglect of this aspect of education in our homes, schools and colleges, is I believe a major one.

Little Foxes

Seldom in my ministry did I have to deal with dramatic fraud or vice, or visit people in prison. But there were numerous occasions when I had to try and resolve disputes between touchy and prickly members, often over matters which in the great scheme of things, were relatively unimportant. Who should or should not be allowed to use the Guild Cups? What colour should the church hall be painted? Which child should present the bouquet of flowers, or carry the Queen's colours at the Remembrance Service? Pettiness and discourtesies often caused considerable tension and upsets. Many a 'kirk' fight stemmed from trigger-quick reactions to minor differences of opinions. I soon learned that principles without politeness, guts without grace, convictions without courtesy, are not enough.

What a strange mixture of saint and sinner we all are. Friends of the Scottish philosopher Thomas Carlyle marvelled at how well he coped when he discovered that his maid had burned his manuscript of the *History of the French Revolution,* a manuscript he had been working on for years. She had thought it was a bundle of waste paper. Yet the same Carlyle often made the lives of his wife and neighbours miserable by his peevish complaints and upsets. On returning from speaking engagements, he often hung up his fiddle at the back door. He was easily irritated. A neighbour's cock crowing early in the morning, infuriated him.

Far more marriages and homes are broken by thoughtlessness, sullenness, fussiness, moodiness, and nagging, than by infidelity. One wife said of her husband, who was an actor, "He was a comedian on the stage, but a tragedian at home." Tetchiness and arrogance continue to wreak havoc in many marriages. Homes would be happier places if the elementary courtesies of life were observed, if before criticising, we tried first to see things from the other's point of view.

Smartphones

Some years ago a man used his mobile phone to ask the operator for the number of the Shell garage in Liverpool. When the operator inquired which one he wanted, as there were several in the Liverpool area, the man said, "The one in which I am locked in the toilet." As well as being of help in emergencies, smartphones and other digital devices let us surf the web and by means of Skype and Facebook keep in close contact with family members and friends.

Alongside the many blessings of digital devices, there are also negative consequences. The Internet has helped turn radical extremist movements into global forces. Youngsters who have become addicted to their smartphone or tablet, are reluctant to be disturbed. On family outings, instead of enjoying the surrounding countryside, or sharing in conversation, youngsters' eyes are focussed on screens.

Professor Sherry Turkle, who for thirty years has studied the psychology of our relationships with technology, entitled her recent book *Reclaiming Conversation.* It has the subtitle, 'The Power of Talk in a Digital Age'. In it she shares some staggering facts, that the average American adult checks the smartphone every six minutes, that many teen-agers sleep with their phones. The moment they wake, they check for messages. They go nowhere without their phones. For them social media is where they feel most at home.

A teenage boy informed his mother one day that he had received a text from his best friend, saying that his father had died suddenly. When he told her that he had texted him back to say he was sorry, his mother, almost uncomprehend-ing, asked, "Why did you not phone and speak to him?" The mother learned that, whereas she believed that conversation was the cornerstone of empathy, the most comforting and humanising thing people can often do, her son thought conversation on such occasions would be intrusive.

Dr Turkle expresses concern about the retreat from face-to-face conversation. She encourages parents to take respon-sibility for the use of technology in the same way as they take responsibility for the food their youngsters eat. She underlines the need for families to make time for conver-sation, to create spaces and times in their home which are free of digital devices, especially at meal times. Her clarion call is for us to lift our eyes from our digital screens, and talk.

McCaig's Folly

Above the seaside town of Oban in the Scottish Highlands is the massive McCaig's tower, built in the pattern of the Roman Coliseum. There were ten McCaig children. All died unmarried. Each left his or her property and money to the others. A goodly sum had accumulated by the late 19th century. About this time the building of the circular tower began. The motivation was the fear that, despite their wealth, the McCaig name might vanish from the face of the earth. The McCaigs hoped that by building this monument on such a prominent site, their name would be remembered for centuries to come. In the great niches of the circular structure, statues of the McCaigs were to be placed. But, as a result of a crown case taken out by the people of Oban against the executors of the McCaig will, the statues were never made, and the tower never completed. Unsoundness of mind was the substance of the crown case. The mental unsoundness was their all-consuming desire to immortalise their name by this monstrous useless structure, known today as McCaig's Folly.

Contrast the McCaigs with one of their contemporaries, William Quarrier, who built a village for orphan children in Bridge of Weir. The stone houses there were comparable in standard to those in the suburbs of any city. Quarrier had a deep concern for underprivileged youngsters. He not only provided food for those wandering aimlessly in the streets and frequenting the Glasgow railway stations, he shared with them his idea of creating a shoe-cleaning brigade. He would provide uniforms, brushes and polish. By day they earned money cleaning shoes. At night they attended classes which Quarrier organised. When you compare the McCaigs investing in massive monuments, with Quarrier investing so much in other lives and good causes, you are struck by the immense difference between those who put themselves at the centre of life, who strive fiercely for distinction, and those who seek to enrich the lives of their contemporaries and the future of generations yet unborn.

Napoleon and Pasteur

Some years ago a poll was taken in France to decide the most distinguished Frenchman of all time. Napoleon, despite his gigantic tomb, and the Arc de Triomphe, his own personal tribute to his military might, did not come near the top of the poll. Number one was the scientist Louis Pasteur, a man who, though partially paralysed, did so much to enrich human life. He not only established the science of bacteriology, but did a vast amount of work to improve French industry and agriculture. It was Pasteur's dedication to the world of pure science and the welfare of humanity which made him such a well-loved figure. The famous Pasteur Institute in Paris still carries on his work on contagious and other diseases. From that well which Pasteur dug, the world still draws benefit. Every time we drink pasteurised milk we stand in his debt.

A study of the history of any country reveals its Napoleons and Pasteurs. Germany had its Kaisers and Hitlers, obsessed with their own power and glory, but Germany also had its George Frederick Handel concerned to enrich the world with great music, and its Dietrich Bonhoeffer, a Lutheran Pastor, executed for his strong opposition to the Nazi regime. America had its Mafia god-fathers, but also its Franklin D Roosevelt, concerned about a new deal for the underprivileged, and its Martin Luther King with his dreams of a more just and brotherly world. Italy had its Caligulas and Neros, but also its Michelangelo concerned to beautify the world with his sculptures and paintings, and its St Francis concerned to sow love where there was hate, faith where there was doubt, light where there was darkness.

The world finally remembers with affection those who serve it. History also finally honours those who seek to enrich and enlarge the lives of others.

Shalom

One morning on Radio 2, Rabbi Neuberger told how a member of the Anglican Church had been present at a Jewish wedding she had conducted. At the reception following the wedding ceremony, he told her how delighted he had been to hear her use in the wedding service, the lovely Christian blessing, "The Lord bless you and keep you ... The Lord lift up the light of his countenance upon you and give you peace." On hearing this Rabbi Neuberger smiled and said, "That blessing was part of our Jewish heritage, thousands of years before the Anglican church used it." She was right.

Shalom, the lovely Jewish word for peace, is so rich in meanings that many different words and phrases are used to translate it. Though it can mean public order, or inner calm, or the absence of friction and war, its deeper meaning is the harmonious function of our whole nature, a sense of wholeness.

People seek peace in different ways. Rich people often seek it through financial security; orthodox religious people seek it by accepting a well defined creed. The poet Tennyson believed we only experience real peace and harmony when "We are loyal to the royal in us." There can be no peace when our minds are dominated by the desire to hurt, or when we allow prejudice to influence our behaviour, or when our actions are motivated by self-interest, envy and greed.

There can be no peace when we ferociously pursue our own sectional interests regardless of the consequences on others. There can be no peace when we exploit the ignorance and weakness of others, or turn deaf ears to the cries of minorities who plead for justice.

When, on his last journey to Jerusalem, Jesus rounded a corner, and saw before him the Holy City with its walls and domes and parapets shimmering in the sunshine, we are told he wept. "Would that you knew the things that make for peace," he said. The corruption of the temple officials, the legalism of the Pharisees, and the racial arrogance and inhumanity of many of his contemporaries, greatly saddened him. It was because Jesus continued to speak out strongly against these things that a few days later he was arrested and crucified. I sometimes wonder if the test of true discipleship is how much we are at odds with many aspects of the world's life and the world's standards.

Leaving Bitterness Behind

No one makes it through life without being hurt, rejected or betrayed. Though in many novels that we read, and dramas that we watch, betrayal often results in the death of the perpetrator of the hurt, most people's revenge is more subtle. It seeps out indirectly in bitter, nasty remarks and seizing every opportunity to hurt as we were hurt, to humiliate as we were humiliated. The outcome is often the breaking off of all contact.

I remember hearing of a Canadian family who became involved in one of those disputes which end in court. The judge ruled in favour of the elder son, whose main evidence consisted of a blatant lie. When the case finished, the younger son wrote to his brother: "I know you are a liar. You know you are a liar. This will rankle with you even more than the possession of the property will gratify you. My only satisfaction is that every morning when you are shaving, you will look in the mirror and know that I know you are a liar." The divided families had no further contact. Two years later the younger son learned from a neighbour that his brother had moved to Kansas City. He was sporting a large beard!

Neither brother had won. As regards peace of mind, sleep and health, both lost heavily. Now I certainly don't condone the older son's lie, but had his brother despite all the psychic pain suffered, been willing to forgive, he would have lost nothing but the trial. His mental and physical health would not have suffered.

The Greek philosopher Epictetus said, "Everything has two handles; by one you carry it, by the other you cannot." He then provided an illustration of what he meant. Suppose your brother has offended you. You may attempt to carry the estrangement by the handle of the injury. If you do, your brooding can only make the offence more bitter. On the other hand you may decide to carry the estrangement, not by the handle of the offence, but by the handle of the relationship. My brother may have offended me; nevertheless he is my brother! If you allow your thought to dwell on that, you may yet be reconciled to your brother.

An Indian snake is reported to be so savage that when it stings, its fangs break and it dies from its own poison.

That is true also of those who nurse bitter grievances. What poison is injected into their soul. Not forgiving is like drinking poison and expecting the other person to die. Sir Walter Scott knew that one of life's greatest tragedies is a person who has developed an obsessive hatred against someone. He described the longing for revenge as "the sweetest morsel to the mouth", but then had the insight to add, "that was ever cooked in hell".

When Nelson Mandela, was released from his lengthy prison sentence, for leading the struggle against apartheid, he was asked if he was bitter about what had happened to him. His moving reply was "If I did not leave my bitterness behind, I would still be in prison."

Curiosity

I love the story of the young camel whose curiosity prompted him to ask his Mummy why she had a hump on her back. His Mummy explained that God gave camels humps so that water could be stored for long journeys across the desert where there was little or no water. When the little camel then asked why she had such big feet, his Mummy explained that camels were given big feet so that they would be able to walk more easily over the sand. The little camel's next question was why did she have such big eye-lashes. The Mummy camel explained that camels were given big eye-lashes so that when the wind blows in the desert, the sand does not get into their eyes. "Mummy," said the little camel, with a puzzled look on his face, "Why then are we in this zoo?"

Curiosity is also a precious and powerful part of the make-up of children. They want explanations of things they do not understand. Though parents are sometimes almost driven mad by their children's endless questions – "Why, why, why?" – asking questions is the way the mind learns and develops. Science stemmed from human curiosity about the mysteries of life and the universe. What a debt we owe to inquiring minds, past and present, men and women who asked: "Why?" Without curiosity the mind becomes dull and goes to sleep. Without curiosity there would be no progress.

Smiles

Though Andrew Marr, the BBC interviewer, has made a good recovery from a major stroke, he now finds it more difficult to smile. In an interview he told how for years he had taken for granted his ability to break his face into a smile. Some years ago an Egyptian boy was brought to Britain to have an operation to his face. The surgeons hoped they could save his smile which he was in danger of losing. Fortunately the operation was a success and he has now returned to Cairo knowing that he will be able to go on smiling.

These two news items got me thinking about this wonderful gift of being able to smile. I often wonder how many romances have been started by a stray smile in the passing. What tremendous joy a baby's first smile gives to her parents. A smile at the right time is one of the best things I know for oiling the machinery of life. I am sorry that the Girl Guides in America no longer have to promise to be cheerful, just courageous and strong, for cheerful smiling people are such a tonic.

Smiling is one of the most powerful and influential forms of communication. It is more than just an outward gesture. There is a lot going on behind our smiles. We smile to indicate we are pleased, or to let people know we agree with what they said. The way people smile also reveals much about them. We can usually tell when a person is smiling for effect. The phoney smile has no real warmth in the eyes. It is also often short-lived. The sunshine smile on the other hand is far more genuine and lasts longer. Characteristics of this smile are a creased up nose and warm eyes. The lips are open and the teeth in full view. Whereas phoney smilers are very concerned about what others think of them, sunshine smilers have a far more carefree attitude. The best smiles are unplanned.

Simple Solutions

Someone once said that to every complex problem there is a simple solution, and that simple solution is usually wrong! Life being complex and full of ambiguities there are often no simple solutions. The problem is heightened by the fact that middle ways are not fashionable with people who want to establish one pole as absolute truth, who think in terms of everything being black or white. Part of the problem is that we have often to balance two opposing truths at the same time.

Imagine a dream in which we are being chased through a tropical forest, swinging in Tarzan-like fashion from one vine to another, dodging arrows from a pursuing tribe, weaving between elaborate traps set by our opponents. Suddenly a great chasm appears in front of us. In one ear we hear a wise voice saying, "Look before you leap." In the other ear we hear another voice saying, "The one who hesitates is lost." We have a problem, for these two contrasting wise pieces of advice set up a real dilemma.

There is no dictionary of conduct to consult for simple answers to complex problems. Wise are those people who, realising the limits of traditional proverbial wisdom, base their decisions on the centrality and superiority of genuine caring concern. Good leadership is dependent on those in positions of authority having sensitive, understanding hearts, hearts skilled at listening to the cries, longings and dreams of people. People need to feel they are being listened to, not merely legislated for or dictated to. The need for sensitive understanding is essential in most professions. I do not want an insensitive doctor who writes a prescription without having really listened to my story. Nor do most people want a church minister who fails to make time to listen to their questions, doubts and fears, or an insensitive teacher who does not make an effort to listen to what is troubling her pupils.

Going Off the Rails

One Sunday the Rev. John Chambers, a retired Inverness minister, had been invited to conduct the morning service in Dornoch Cathedral. That day he began his talk to the children by saying, "I am old, I am very old, so old that I cannot remember what primary school was like." On hearing this a wee boy shouted out, "Well sir, it is awful!"

Though I too am old, I can remember my primary school days. Though they were during the Second World

War, I have warm, not awful, memories of them. Each day we took to school, along with our school bag, a gas mask, knitting needles and wool. With the latter we knitted squares to be sewn into blankets for the soldiers.

Though we had no mobile phones, iPads, or even television, we did have a huge and wonderful area of open ground behind our house. There we played football, cricket and ran races. Running through this vast play area was a disused railway line, used formerly to transport quality stone from the Giffnock quarry, to build some of Glasgow's finest buildings. We sometimes had a competition to see how far we could walk on the rails without falling off.

One day two older boys joined us. They boasted they could walk further on the rails than we could. Accepting their challenge, we went first. Focussing on the rail we thought we did well. We never thought they would beat us, but they did. One of them got on one railway line and the other on the second line. Joining arms, they supported each other as they walked! Though at the time we were sure they had cheated, I often later in life recalled this incident on observing people whose lives had been derailed because they had focussed solely on themselves and their own advancement.

In the film *The Imitation Game*, the mathematical genius tells a story of how friends were walking in the jungle when they hear the roar of a lion. One starts thinking of places they can hide. The second puts on his running shoes. When the first says, "You cannot possibly run faster than the lion," the second replies, "I don't need to run faster than the lion. I just need to run faster than you." This highlights the human dilemma. Which comes first? The common good or individual self-interest?

Life has taught me that those who learn early in life to think in terms of we rather than I, who seek to support others as well as themselves, are far less likely to go off the rails.

❦

The Beadle

In Scotland the term "Beadle" has an interesting history. The word is a contraction of the Latin word "Bedellus" which was used to designate the person whose duty it was to summon parties before a public court. In the 17th and 18th centuries, one of the main roles of church beadles was to issue citations to those not attending church, or suspected of lying or committing adultery. These citations were summons to appear before the all powerful Kirk Session.

Kirk Session minutes of that period are full of censorious judgments and penalties passed on parishioners for their misdemeanours. Those found guilty were handed over to the beadle for punishment. Clothed in cloaks of coarse linen, they had, on a Sunday, to sit on the repentance stool, placed in front of the pulpit, 'that creepy chair' as Robert Burns called it.

Another responsibility of beadles was to open and shut the church doors and ring the bell calling parishioners to worship. With serious face they took the Bible and Psalter up into the pulpit, before leading in the minister with measured and dignified tread. Dr Archie Craig, a distinguished Moderator of the Church of Scotland in the 1960s, told how during his student days he had been asked to conduct worship in an Aberdeenshire church. On his arrival the beadle, clad in black suit and bow tie, went over the procedure for entry into the sanctuary. "I will go first with the Bible and you will follow at a respectful distance!"

Beadles also had the responsibility of maintaining discipline during the observance of public worship, of quietening noisy children and wakening those who had fallen asleep during what were often lengthy sermons. It was the beadle's responsibility to turn the hour glass if it ran down before the minister finished his sermon! In the Session records of a Perth church we are told the beadle had "a red staff wherewith to waken sleepers." Beadles were regularly called on by the minister to fulfil many other duties. In the 19th century, behind Langside Free Church there was a sloping field. One Sunday a cow took her place close to the church. At the close of the psalm before the sermon, the cow raised her own voice to such an extent that the minister stopped his sermon, and told the beadle to chase the cow away. Most beadles responded positively when called on by the minister to do something, but not all. One beadle on being instructed by a visiting preacher to waken those sleeping, said, "Sir, you put them to sleep, so you can waken them up."

More Beadle Humour

Beadles were renowned for their forthright and often not very flattering comments. "If your text had had scarlet fever," said one to a guest preacher, "your sermon would not have caught it." After preaching as a candidate for the vacancy, a young minister retired to the vestry where he derobed. Anxious to learn more about what he hoped would be the scene of his future labours, he returned to the church where he found the beadle clearing up. "I am just taking a look at the church," observed the candidate in a casual sort of way. "Aye, take a good look at it, for it is not likely you will ever see it again."

I remember hearing how one New Year's day, which happened to fall on a Sunday, the Helmsdale beadle staggered into the Free Church for the evening service at the end of the opening Psalm. When the minister later inquired what had delayed him, he replied that he had been up the Strath that afternoon, and that in each house he had been given his New Year. "Look," said the minister, "I too was visiting up the strath this afternoon and I am not in the state you are." "Aye," said the beadle, "but you are not as popular as me."

In country parishes in the old days, the beadle often had to look after the manse garden, plough the manse glebe, feed the cows, sell the sheep, buy the lambs, and sometimes dig graves. The beadle of Kilwinning Church also had the responsibility of showing visitors round the old Abbey Church. For doing this he was often recompensed. On one occasion, however, when a lady at the end of the tour offered him only words of thanks, the wily beadle replied, "My lady, when you go home, if you find out that you have lost your purse, you will at least remember you have not had it out here."

The 19th-century writer Nicholas Dickson tells of John Gowdie, a fine specimen of a beadle, who fell in love with Katie, the minister's housekeeper. One night when John suggested that she might go for a stroll with him, instead of taking her along one of the area's many picturesque walks, he took her to the churchyard. Pointing to a spot in the cemetery, he said, "My folk lie there. Would you like one day to lie there too?" His most unusual 'grave' marriage proposal was accepted!

Throughout my ministry, I was fortunate to have beadles who had less austere faces than many of their predecessors. In Shakespeare's lovely phrase about Desdemona, they held it a vice in their goodness not to do more than they have to. Because of the way Jock Maclean, one of the Dornoch Cathedral beadles, walked, he had acquired the nickname Jock Frog. When word reached the local pub that Jock had been the successful candidate for the post of beadle, a local wit was overheard to say, "The age of miracles is not dead. God has just transformed a frog into a beetle."

Language

Language is not a trivial issue. It enables us to express perceptions and make distinctions. It is the chief means we have of showing people respect or contempt, understanding or indifference. To say that a person is short and another tall, one young and another old, one dark and another fair, is to make neutral observations. But once we begin to identify one characteristic as desirable and another as undesirable, one as the norm and one the exception, prejudice enters the picture. People have long felt there is something peculiar about those who are in some respect different. An old Highlander once said to his friend, "All the world is peculiar except thee and me, and sometimes I think thee a little peculiar."

Language reveals people's cultural, national, racial or religious biases. Long ago many city dwellers regarded country folk with contempt. Whereas city life was thought to be associated with refinement, not so rural life. City folk often used the derogatory word 'villain' to describe inferior country dwellers, many of whom were employed as servants at villas. Villa was the Latin word for a large country house. Thankfully many offensive terms from the past are now seldom heard.

Left-handed

Today few people think there is anything strange about people being left-handed. But that has not always been the case. For centuries, many thought left-handed people could not be trusted. They were deviant and somehow dangerous. The word 'sinister', meaning threatening or evil, comes from the Latin word for left. Over the years the word acquired ominous overtones. It was no different with *gauche*, the French word for left. It entered our language meaning awkward and clumsy. On the other hand, *dexter*, the Latin word for right, gave us the word dexterous, meaning skilful. In Anglo-Saxon *lyft* meant weak and useless. The German word for left, *links*, meant clumsy or awkward. In Spanish *izquierdo* meant not only left, but crooked. If in Russia you operate *nalyevo*, on the left, you are the kind of person who is willing to take bribes. The impression is still given that what is good in Western culture is right, not left. We still talk about a celebrity's right-hand man, and left-handed compliments.

In the past if children started writing left-handed, teachers and parents would sometimes tie their left hand behind their back, forcing them to write right-handed.

Fortunately that no longer happens. For a period in Britain there was a society called "The Society for Justice for the Left-handed." I am told that at one stage they considered calling it "Rights for the Left-handed!" Their aim included getting left-handed desks and scissors for schools, and to pressurise industry into making left-handed tools.

Though modern translations of the Bible, and compilers of hymn books have worked hard on inclusive language, the hymn, "O brother man, fold to thy heart thy brother ..." being rewritten as "Children of God reach out to one another", the church continues to talk of extending to new members the 'right' hand of fellowship, and of the risen Christ as sitting 'at the right hand of God.'

Huckleberry Finn

History records fearful crimes committed in the name of conscience. An historian says of King Philip II of Spain, that he "inflicted more suffering in obedience to conscience than the Emperors Nero and Domitian in obedience to their lusts." Shakespeare wrote of 'a conscience wide as Hell.' Jesus spoke of the inner light which can become dark. In George Orwell's *1984*, Big Brother, using the technique of the 'Big Lie', succeeds in making people believe "War is peace, freedom is slavery and ignorance is strength". Those who crucified Jesus acted according to the dictates of their consciences.

The influences that surround us from our earliest years, the outlook, values and prejudices of our parents, the promises of threats and rewards, influence the demands our consciences lay on us. Freud believed that even when parents are no longer around to deter us from wrong actions, our 'super-ego' has become conditioned to act in their stead. This he believed explained the guilt-feelings and sleepless nights we experience when we act contrary to the standards of our parents and community.

From childhood, Huckleberry Finn was taught that slaves were their owners' property. Negro Jim and his children were the property of Miss Watson who had bought Jim as a slave. When Jim ran away, Huck's conditioned conscience nagged him because he did not tell Miss Watson where Jim was. When he heard Jim speak of trying to get his own children back, again Huck's conscience nagged him, for according to what he had been taught, that would be stealing. But because of some wider feeling of human decency, which he could not fully identify, he felt that what was accepted as right, was in fact wrong.

Life would have been easier for Dietrich Bonhoeffer and Martin Niemöller, who were imprisoned for speaking out against Hitler, had they dismissed the demands of their consciences. Florence Nightingale need not have gone to nurse wounded soldiers in Crimea. Her own family called her crazy for considering it. But there was a 'have-to' inside her. This 'have to' led the philosopher Kant to exclaim that nothing was more inspiring than the starry heavens above and the moral law within.

More Honest than Most

During my year as Moderator of the Church of Scotland, my wife and I lived in Charlotte Square in Edinburgh, in a flat which a hundred years before had been the home of the outstanding Scottish preacher Dr Alexander Whyte. For a few years Dr Whyte had as his young assistant, Hugh Black, who later became a professor of preaching in New York. It was jokingly said that whereas Dr Whyte in his sermons black-balled the saints, Hugh Black white-washed the sinners. As time passed, Hugh, who had caught the ear of the younger generation, began drawing even larger congregations than Dr Whyte. Whyte once confided to a friend what problems that caused him. Knowing how loyal Dr Whyte was to his assistant, the friend said he had difficulty believing that. "Ah," said Dr Whyte, "you don't know the black depths of the human heart." Alexander Whyte was more honest than most.

We all have to deal with four types of people –

• those less prosperous and less able;

• those with whom we have many things in common, but whom we surpass in a few things;

• those who have certain things in common with us, but in other things surpass us;

• those who far excel us.

It is the third group, those who have been running alongside us, but suddenly forge ahead, that constitute the critical moral problem, those who pip us at the post, who get the promotion or praise we covet, those whose income now allows designer clothes, a luxury car and exotic holidays, or those whose children at school get better grades. Most people understand what Shakespeare was getting at when he wrote,

The General's disdained by him one step below, he by the next, that next by him beneath; so every step.

To bring ourselves to say of another what John the Baptist said of Jesus, when some of his followers left him to become followers of Jesus, "He must become more important, while I become less important", is one of life's hardest battles. Perhaps it was his amazing lack of envy that led Jesus to say, "Among those born of women there is not a greater than John the Baptist."

Eyeing Others

"Such men as he be never at heart's ease while they behold a greater than themselves." So said Shakespeare's Julius Caesar about Cassius. Seventy years ago Bertrand Russell, the brilliant British mathematician and philosopher, was about as famous as anyone in the English-speaking world, yet his friend Gerald Brenan tells us that Russell was upset because he was not as well-known or as highly regarded as Albert Einstein.

With what loathing envy often eyes the more capable person. As a result of slaying Goliath, David became a national hero. King Saul appointed him a leader in the army. In that capacity David's exploits had a strong popular appeal. As the years passed Saul became fiercely envious of David's accomplishments and popularity. The Jewish women chanted, "Saul has slain his thousands, but David his ten thousands." That riled Saul. The author of the Book of Samuel tells us that Saul eyed David.

In a world that maximises envy we seldom hear people pass scrupulously fair judgments about those who surpass them, or have things they would love to have. To what terrible lengths envy, the sin of the 'have nots' against the 'haves', can drive people. How often it has resulted in plotting another's downfall. Pilate was insightful enough to know that it was out of envy that the Jewish religious leaders wanted to put Jesus to death.

The Italian painter Giotto depicted envy with large distended ears, a creature eager to hear anything bad about a worthier neighbour. Envy being closely linked with greed, Giotto portrays envy as clutching a bag of gold in one hand and reaching out with the other, his fingers sharpened to claws. Envy also being very cunning, Giotto pictures a serpent springing from envy's mouth. But there is still more to envy, and Giotto knew it. He depicts the monster living in self-torture. The serpent's fangs fasten on envy's own brow. The flames about his feet are about to burn him and his world. No wonder envy is listed among the seven deadly sins.

Success and Failure

The axiom, "If at first you don't succeed try, try again", has become so engrained in our psyche, that some mistakenly believe that failure is always the result of not trying hard enough. How mistaken that is. Failure, as the world conceives it, is a word found not only in the dictionary of fools and cowards, but of many fine people. Addressing students at St Andrews University J. M. Barrie, the author of *Peter Pan*, reminded them that, "We are all failures – at least the best of us are." When Thomas Edison was challenged about his hundreds of failed attempts to perfect the light bulb, he said, "I keep discovering other ways of not inventing the electric light bulb." Churchill expressed it well. "Success is not final. Failure is not fatal. It is the courage to continue that counts."

Dr Peter Doherty, the winner of the Nobel Prize for Medicine in 1996 writes, "In scientific research, the public hears only of grand accomplishments. Untold years of toil, dead ends, wild goose chases all pock the road to great scientific achievements ... Success in scientific research is built on failure. If you don't fail, you are not trying to do anything new. The scientific method requires that you struggle to disprove or falsify your best ideas ... We scientists are rather accustomed to falling flat on our faces. The course of science and understanding depends on getting up where failure has left us."

Had Moses' obituary been written the day after he died, before reaching the Promised Land, he would probably have been deemed a failure. The majority of those he had freed from slavery in Egypt were convinced that, far from making their conditions better, he had in fact made them worse. His story is a powerful reminder that apparent failure in the eyes of the world does not necessarily mean failure in the sight of God. Moses' forty-year tireless struggle for his recalcitrant people was in fact his glory.

In the 19th century Father Damien cast in his lot with the leper community on the island of Molokai. He became the physician of their souls and bodies, their teacher, carpenter, gardener, cook and even grave-digger. After twelve strenuous years Damien himself contracted and finally died of the dreaded disease, leaving few worldly possessions. Was Damien a failure? The Belgian people did not think so. A few years ago they voted him the greatest Belgian of all time.

The Royal and Ancient Game

The tie of the Royal and Ancient Golf Club at St Andrews, the Vatican of golf, depicts St Andrew bearing the X-shaped cross on which he was crucified. I cannot help wondering if it is because so many golfers suffer so many agonies and disappointments on the golf course that golf's governing body decided to choose as their emblem the figure of a tortured saint.

Had I been more honest I would probably have admitted in my late teens and twenties that golf was often more pain than fun. How mistaken my young wife was in thinking that every time I was on the golf course I was having enormous fun. Though at the end of a medal round, I would often make light of my score, in the dark corners of my ego, it hurt. Fortunately by the time I moved to Dornoch, the mental anguish associated with the game had lessened. The lined and anxious face and the furrowed golfing brow, were now for the most part gone. The friendship of fellow golfers, and the light-hearted banter associated with the game became far more important. If it was an enjoyable match with friends, I regarded myself as being the winner, even if I lost.

The pleasure associated then with the Royal and Ancient game was also greatly increased by being able to play on such a high-quality and challenging course as Royal Dornoch. Even if the drives were not flying as straight or as far as I might have liked, and the putts were not always dropping, the panoramic views of the sandy beaches and the Sutherland hills, and the fresh sea breezes, compensated considerably.

Golf strengthens flabby muscles. Golfers who reach three score years and ten are generally fitter than non-golfers of the same age. Golf affords healthy exercise for all, sufficient for the young, and yet not too strenuous for the retired. Golf is a game for players of all ages, for lads and lassies of 8 to 18, but also for swinging octogenarians. Samuel Ryder, of Ryder Cup fame, and the distinguished broadcaster Alistair Cooke were past fifty when they took up golf. Though neither became all that proficient at the game, they found it a most pleasant way of spending leisure hours. Quickly succumbing to the lure of the game, golf became Alistair Cooke's great sporting passion. He played well into his nineties, even though by that time his drives were so short that he could 'hear the ball land'!

I have never owned the secret of great golf. I have just been grateful when I was occasionally allowed to borrow it for a short time. More than 70 years playing the game has taught me that the only two shots I am ever likely to master completely are the practice swing and the conceded putt. Fortunately as well as levelling down golf also levels up. Part of the fascination of the game is that every so often even happy hackers can play shots or sink putts that would delight a Rory McIlroy. Every moment of golfing ecstasy is worth hours of golfing agony.

Golf and Character

In many respects golf is an X-ray of the soul. President Taft, a former President of the United States, said of the Royal and Ancient Game, "There is nothing that furnishes a greater test of character and self-restraint than golf, nothing that puts one more on an equality with one's fellows, or may I say puts one lower than one's fellows than the game of golf. If there is anything which will instil in one's heart a more intense feeling of self-abasement and humiliation than the game of golf, I should like to know what it is." Golf is a game in which mental attitude is more important than physical strength. It is a real test of temper, honour and character.

Hale Irwin might have protested that the fresh air putt which cost him the coveted British Open title, was really an attempt to remove an insect from the top of his ball. But he immediately informed the referee that he had attempted to hit the ball. When something similar happened to Bobby Jones in the American Open, he immediately called a penalty on himself. When later praised for this, he said, "Look, there is only one way to play golf. You might as well praise a man for not robbing a bank." The St Andrews caddie was right when he said, "Golf is a grand game for letting you see what is in a man." The grunts, squeaks and mutterings, the whooping and bellowing and other audio disturbances of a golfer, when a crazy bounce or kick, or some other ill-fortune, puts his ball into deep trouble, can reveal facets of a person's character unknown before.

A visitor to Dornoch, a gentleman of considerable standing, was once heard having an animated conversation with his ball, which had been deflected into one of the deep bunkers guarding the second hole. After several unsuccessful attempts to get it out, he finished up committing the poor soulless thing to imperishable flames! Sam Snead once said of a fellow professional "He was the most even-tempered golfer I ever saw. He was mad all the time." We all know such golfers. Their putters spend more time in the air than Lindbergh ever did.

In other ways golf is a great revealer of character. After a good first nine holes in a competition, some golfers immediately tighten up, imagining all the disasters that could overtake them in the inward half. Other golfers have a tendency to exaggerate, or more euphemistically, to 'think big' – to overestimate the length of their drives by at least 20 yards; to make the best shot they ever made in their life several times a year and lie about the awful lies they had. Many who say they shoot in the low eighties average one round out of twenty below ninety.

The Golfing Prince

During my time as captain of Royal Dornoch Golf Club, the most northerly of Scotland's championship golf courses, I had the privilege of partnering Prince Andrew. In the warm summer sunshine, the Dornoch course and the surrounding countryside looked their very best. A victory that day over the club secretary and professional greatly added to our enjoyment!

Two years later Prince Andrew and I were invited to join the golf commentator Peter Alliss in a televised golf match, as part of a BBC series about golf in remote corners of the world. On that occasion, the Dornoch weather could not have been worse. There was no let-up in the torrential rain. The programme began with Peter Alliss, cowering under a large golf-umbrella on the first tee, saying, "My mother said there would be days like this." Afterwards, over a cup of warm coffee in the clubhouse, the conversation took an interesting turn. It did not focus on the horrendous weather, or the world famous golfers like Tom Watson, Greg Norman and Ben Crenshaw, who had played Royal Dornoch. Instead Peter Alliss told us how as a young man he had been put off the church by a few insufferable 'holier than thou' people he had met. Prince Andrew responded by telling how the previous week a rather pious gentleman, who had been sitting next to his mother at a London banquet, asked her if she was "a real Christian". The Queen, who has a very deep Christian faith, was understandably taken aback by the question.

In the fascinating clubhouse discussion which ensued, I shared with them a story, the story of a boy walking on the beach with his father. Seeing a rainbow striking the rocks at the end of the beach, he said, "Dad, I want to go and stand in the light of the rainbow." Even though he ran as hard as he could, the rainbow kept receding. But when the wee lad reached the rocks, his father saw *him* bathed in the light of the rainbow. That for me is a parable. The older I become, the more aware I become of my own shortcomings and alternating moods. The goal keeps receding. I am not the Christian I had hoped I would be. But I press on, hoping that, just possibly, others might glimpse in my actions and hear in my words, something of the Galilean accent.

The Shadow We Cast

In the early 19th century the Rev. James Smith emigrated from Dundee to America. There he became the minister of a church in Springfield, Illinois, where the young Abraham Lincoln was practising law. Lincoln and his wife first met the Rev. Smith when their second son Edward died at the age of three from tuberculosis. Shortly after the funeral, they became worshippers in his church. Abraham and his wife Mary were so impressed with their Scottish minister, his thoughtful preaching and the scholarly treatise he had written on the Christian faith, that shortly after Lincoln's assassination, as a token of the President's esteem and affection, the family arranged for him to receive one of the President's gold-headed canes.

It is doubtful if James Smith ever realised the impact that his faithful ministry had made on the future President, and through Lincoln on the world. In many of Lincoln's oft-quoted sayings one can detect the influence of the faith and honest questioning of the Rev. Smith. "There is much I do not understand," said Lincoln, "but I have an overpowering sense of the part God has for me to play in His world, to the end that His will might somehow get itself done, to some degree at least through me." Convinced that slavery was irreconcilable with justice and humanity, he sought to persuade his political colleagues that God had decided the question of slavery in favour of the slaves.

Though Lincoln was an unprepossessing and ungainly figure and came from lowly origins, like a plain wire in a radiator which has become incandescent, his humility, integrity, love of liberty, and his deep faith, which had been nurtured by the Rev. Smith, made a profound impact. Lincoln knew that those who perform great acts as though they were small, and small acts as though they were great, bring many blessings to the world. A kindly smile, a word of appreciation or reassurance, a courageous intervention can have a chain of consequences far beyond our imagining.

We can no more live in the world without influencing others than we can walk in the sun and not cast a shadow.

Effective and Affected

Though as a trainee minister I was told that I must learn to confront grievous situations unemotionally, I never learned that art. It might have saved emotional wear and tear, but there would have been much less pastoral comfort. I don't want a doctor, nurse, neighbour or minister who is coldly dispassionate in the presence of my pain. I want professionals and neighbours who really care. If we are to be effective, we cannot avoid being affected.

In refugee camps where clothing and food are scarce, mothers are often found shivering and emaciated, denying themselves that their children might benefit. That typifies motherhood at its noblest – sainthood without a halo. When Sir James Simpson, the discoverer of chloroform, (no relation unless, perhaps, as a friend once suggested, "Both of you are good at putting people to sleep!") was searching for a simple anaesthetic, he spent the summer of 1847 trying out various chemical compounds on himself. Wanting to save others pain, he risked damaging his own health.

If Lord Shaftesbury had not made himself so unpopular with the employers of his day, by taking up the cause of factory workers, he would have safeguarded his good name and probably become Prime Minister. Shortly before his assassination, Martin Luther King, who at great personal cost did so much for the black people in America said, "Longevity has its place. But I am not concerned with that.

I have seen the promised land. I may not get there, but my people will get there."

The wealthy industrialist Charles Schwab was once involved in a petty lawsuit, brought by a young man he had been trying to help. To the surprise of the media, instead of sending a highly paid lawyer to represent him, he decided to appear in his own defence. The plaintiff was obviously seeking notoriety, and he thought some easy money. In concluding his testimony Charles Schwab said, "I want to say that many of my troubles have been caused by trying to help other people." Then turning to those in the courtroom he said, "If you want to avoid trouble be hard-boiled. Say no to everybody. You will then walk through life unmolested, but," and here a smile lit up his face, "you won't experience much joy or inner satisfaction."

Harvest

American visitors to Dornoch often marvelled at our harvest thanksgiving services. We went in for them in a big way, decorating the Cathedral, not just with a chaste bowl of flowers, but piling the fruits of the farm, field and garden in the chancel and the doorways. And the singing! Men and women who never ploughed up anything, except perhaps the golf course, expanded their lungs to proclaim, "We plough the fields and scatter", or the more modern version, "We plough the field with tractors, with drills we sow the land".

The gifts of fruit and flowers were greatly appreciated by many in care homes. The monetary contributions were given to Christian Aid to help starving people in those parts of the world where harvests had failed for lack of rain or too much rain.

In an essay about the weather, a 10-year-old girl once spelt rain, Rane. Her teacher, with a twinkle in her eye, said, "That is the worst spell of rain I have seen for some time!" My heart bleeds for those farmers whose crops are ruined by torrential rain or swollen rivers. I often marvel at their stoical and occasionally witty responses. One farmer's wife, who was being rowed away from her flooded farmhouse, when asked how she felt about what had happened, replied, "Well, a few weeks ago a fortune-teller told me that soon I would be going on a cruise. Little did I know it would be in a rowing boat floating down my own driveway."

To a large extent people make their own inside weather. We have all known bright cheery people who have come through very dark and stormy days, and unhappy people who have never had a day's illness, or a major setback.

Four-legged Friends

A man once e-mailed the manager of a small hotel inquiring about the possibility of staying there for a few days. "My wife and I have a well groomed and well behaved dog. Would it be possible to keep him in the bedroom overnight?"

The reply he received read, "All the years I have been running this hotel, I have never had a dog steal towels, bedclothes or pictures off the wall. I have never had to evict a dog for being drunk and disorderly. Your dog is certainly welcome. And if your dog will vouch for you, you are welcome to stay at the hotel too!"

I sometimes wish we human beings shared some of the virtues of our four-legged friends, their unflinching loyalty and readiness to overlook our occasional forgetfulness without resentment, the ecstatic happiness they derive from simple pleasures and everyday happenings – like the announcement of a walk, a pat on the head, the gift of a dog biscuit. Whereas a teenager or friend may break our hearts, or forget or neglect us, a dog will stand by us in good days and bad, in sickness as well as health. Once a dog gives you its love, nothing will shake or diminish it. A dog befriends us with the kind of love that human beings would do well to imitate.

Rebellious Teenagers

Few things are more beautiful than a sunrise, except when you are waiting for a teenager to come home. A close friend told me how one Friday night he got out of bed about two o'clock in the morning to remonstrate with his teenage son who had just returned home. But before he could say anything, his son said, "Dad if you are going to give me a row, first go and put your teeth in."

Raising teenagers is part joy and part guerrilla warfare. The one thing they wear out faster than shoes, is parents. No wonder many parents, during school holidays, pack up their troubles and send them off to summer camps!

A few years before leaving home is feasible, there develops in many teenagers a longing for increasing independence. They stop hanging on their parents' every word. They also stop thinking their mother is one of the most wonderful women in the world and their father one of the wisest men. When teenagers need their homes most, frustration and rebellion begin to mount. If their parents want them to do something, they almost feel obliged to do something else. Many parents would sympathise with the man who said that there are three ways to get something done – do it yourself, hire someone or forbid your teenagers to do it. One father, at his tether end with his teenage son, was heard to say to his wife, "I cannot believe that out of 100,000 sperm, he was the quickest."

Unless families understand what is happening, how the parent's impulse to protect is clashing with the young person's longing to be independent, it can be a stressful time all round, with regular arguments, scenes and occasional rebellions Physically and emotionally teenagers are part adult, part child. With limited knowledge they have to try and appear knowledgeable. Often their feelings are too impulsive to be handled with sophistication. Girls at this stage are very concerned about their appearance. Their bodies are too hurriedly grown to be managed gracefully. Though adolescent boys would not admit it, deep down they are often anxious whether they will be able to carry off their role as men in the world.

Such anxieties sometimes make teenagers so mad that whenever friction surfaces, they reproach their parents with all the indignation they can muster. I am certain the friction could be eased if parents were to recall the emotional turmoil of their adolescence. They would be more likely to respond, not with the "After all we have done for you" attitude, but with greater understanding. For lack of this, many a home becomes a battleground.

True Patriotism

During the opening ceremony of the Glasgow Commonwealth Games in 2014, some words of Robert Burns were projected on to the huge screen. "With joy unfeigned brothers and sisters meet." These words perfectly summed up the friendly and very successful Glasgow games. The majority of the spectators being Scottish, the applause not surprisingly rose considerably as the tartan clad Scottish team entered the arena on the opening night, and as Scottish athletes went on to win many gold medals.

> *God gave all men earth to love,*
> *But since our hearts are small*
> *Ordained for each one spot should prove*
> *Beloved over all*

Patriotism is woven out of a thousand strands of fond memories and associations. It is found among all peoples. Love for one's homeland is as natural and normal as love of home and family. Writing during a period of enforced exile from Jerusalem, the Psalmist wrote, "By the waters of Babylon we sat down and wept, when we remembered Zion."

Jerusalem was where his life's bearings met, a place that had spiritual and psychological coordinates as well as geographical coordinates.

True patriotism is a lovely thing, but it can quickly turn sour. Some of the builders of the British Empire treated whole races of mankind as if by an act of God they belonged to a lower order of creation. One thinks of the inhumanity of the West African slave trade, and of how in Australia and

America, little or no effort was made to co-exist peacefully with the Aborigines or the Native Americans. Thousands of Indians were callously uprooted from their fertile plains. What disdain there was in General Sheridan's remark, "The only good Indians I ever saw were dead ones." How ironical that in the thinking of many of my generation, the Indians were 'the baddies' and the white settlers were 'the goodies'.

Such racial and national conceit was also a dominant characteristic of Nazism. The Nazis were probably the most patriotic people who ever lived! Hitler sought to hijack the 1936 Olympic Games to prove the superiority of the German 'master race'. When a black man Jesse Owens ran faster and jumped further than the German athletes, Hitler stormed out of the arena. Hitler's actions stemmed from his racial assumption that other races were inferior to the Germans. It was to make more room for the 'master race' that he invaded Poland. What pain and suffering his sick nationalism spawned.

Fanatical nationalism and deep rooted religious prejudices are still the greatest dangers confronting our world today. They continue to make for division, strife and war. When Dr Samuel Johnson described patriotism as 'the last refuge of the scoundrel', I am sure he was referring, not to patriotism, but to a false nationalism. I am proud of being Scottish. I rejoice in all that is noble in our history, tradition and achievements, and yet I must never forget that our own nation is only half the truth.

Weeping

When Bishop Tutu, the South African church leader was asked how he would like to be remembered, he replied, "I hope people will say, he loved, he laughed, he cried." One can learn a great deal about people from what causes them to cry. Sometimes people weep for joy. I think of the tears shed by successful candidates in television contests. I think of tears shed by mothers and grandmothers at weddings and graduation ceremonies. How often at prizegivings, fathers have gulped or blown their noses, secretly hoping no one noticed.

Others weep to draw attention to themselves. Just as there are laughs that have the sound of counterfeit coins, so there are counterfeit tears. Occasionally at funerals, I have suspected that behind the crocodile tears, there was little genuine mourning.

Yet others use tears to get their own way. In old 'Westerns', the hero would often start to shuffle when the heroine's eyes filled with tears. "All right, Miss Betsy. I will take you through Apache country, for I just can't stand to see a woman cry." Closely linked to such crying are the tears that flow when people are not invited to a party, or omitted from a vote of thanks, or from a will. Too often, where there is a will, there is a wail!

There is also the weeping associated with human parting. Such tears are physical signs that our sadness has to do with flesh and blood, with one our hands have touched and our hearts have loved. In his poem 'Ae Fond Kiss', Robert Burns writes,

> *Had we never lov'd sae kindly,*
> *Had we never lov'd sae blindly,*
> *Never met or never parted,*
> *We had ne'er been broken-hearted.*

One explanation given for women living, on average, longer than men, is that women are more open about expressing their feelings. Men spend a lot of energy concealing their real feelings. Yet we are told Jesus wept when his friend Lazarus died. So did King David when his son Absalom was killed. When Mohammed's faithful slave Said died, Said's daughter was amazed at seeing the prophet in tears. When she asked, "What do I see?" he replied, "You see a friend weeping over his friend."

Vital Cargo

John Masefield's poem 'Cargoes' was one my generation learned at school. When I was able to recite it, I did not understand its deeper meaning. Now when I think I understand it, I can no longer recite it. In his famous poem Masefield examines different historical periods, and what each regarded as vitally important.

The first verse describes what King Solomon regarded as vital cargo

Quinquireme of Nineveh from distant Ophir
Rowing home to haven in sunny Palestine
With a cargo of ivory,
And apes and peacocks,
Sandalwood, cedarwood, and sweet white wine.

During his reign, Solomon's ships brought back to Palestine, hewn stones, ivory and the finest ornamental timbers. With them he built a great temple that would hopefully convey something of the majesty of God. The ships also brought jewelled plumed peacocks, monkeys and apes, an endless source of delight to children. It is significant that when Solomon's reputation for wisdom was at its highest, he regarded such beautiful and exciting things as vital cargo. He knew that we need things to lift our spirits.

In the days of Queen Elizabeth I, precious stones and gold, most of them plundered, were regarded by many as all-important

Stately Spanish galleon coming from the Isthmus,
Dipping through the Tropics by the palm-green shores,
With a cargo of diamonds,
Emeralds, amethysts,
Topazes, and cinnamon, and gold moidores.

Women played little part in 16th-century public life. Having little else to interest them, the prime concern of the better off was with outward adornment. Gold and jewels were indicative of a woman's worth and her place on the social ladder.

The final verse describes what Masefield regarded as the most striking characteristic of the late 19th century.

Dirty British coaster with a salt-caked smoke stack
Butting through the channel in the mad March days,
With a cargo of Tyne coal,
Road-rail, pig-lead,
Firewood, iron-ware and cheap tin trays.

Manufactured goods had begun to hold undisputed sway in people's lives. It is little different two hundred years later. Many still spend money they cannot afford, purchasing things they do not really need, to impress people, some of whom they do not really like.

For Better or Worse

According to Peter Ustinov, marriage is a three-speed gearbox: affection, friendship and love. It is not advisable to crash your gears and go right through to love straight away. You need to ease your way through. The basis of love is respect, and that needs to be learned from affection and friendship.

❧

Erich Segal, the author of *Love Story*, advises, "True love comes quietly, without banners or flashing lights. If you hear bells, get your ears examined."

❧

A successful marriage requires falling in love many times, always with the same person.

❧

Marriage is a honeycomb into which each partner must put more honey than he takes out.

❧

When a wife laughs at her husband's jokes, they are either good jokes or she's a good wife.

❧

A teacher tells how she has never forgotten how her class was working on Father's Day cards. She had suggested that they could illustrate the card with something their father liked a lot. On hearing this, one wee lad called Gus raised his hand: "May I draw a picture of my mother? My Dad likes her a lot."

❧

A Jill and Don Ross love to recall how they met. Jill had gone to a restaurant where Don was singing. After hearing a song she loved, Jill clapped exuberantly. "I am glad you turned up tonight," Don crooned. When he then asked her if she was married, Jill flirted. "No. Will you sing at my wedding?" "I'll sing at our wedding," he replied, surprising even himself. Seven months later Don kept his promise.

❧

In response to the question "Where would men be today were it not for women?" the reply came, "They would be in the garden of Eden eating water-melon and taking it easy."

❧

A classified advertisement read: "White wedding dress, size ten with veil: £250. Name of available groom upon request."

❧

A lad in a Glasgow pub told his pals how on his 12th wedding anniversary he told his wife that he would take her to the cinema. "But then I blew it by suggesting that we go and see 'Twelve Years a Slave'."

❧

An Atlanta taxi-driver tells how he once took a hiker to Springer, which is at the start of the very arduous 2,100-mile Appalachian Trail. Three days later the man phoned him from Woody Gap, saying he wanted to go home, that the trail was much harder than he had expected. Could he come and collect him? Two days later the man phoned the taxi-driver explaining that his wife insisted that having spent a fortune on the equipment for the walk, she was not going to allow him to quit so easily, so could he drive him back to Woody Gap. The taxi driver again obliged. A few days later he again received a call from the man wanting to be driven to the nearest airport. When the taxi-driver asked, "What about your wife?" he said, "This time I am not going home!"

🌹

A shop assistant tells of a husband who spent almost half-an-hour searching for the right card for their wedding anniversary. When she finally asked him if there was a problem with the selection, the man replied ruefully, "Yes. I cannot find one my wife will believe."

🌹

A couple who had been married for 45 years had nine children and twenty grandchildren. When the wife was asked one day what had been the secret of their staying together all that time, she said, "Many years ago we made a promise to each other – the first one to leave has to take all the kids."

A man was overheard saying to his friend at a football match, "My wife thinks I put football before marriage, even though we have just celebrated our third season together."

🌹

If a marital disagreement starts with the words, "What did you mean by that?" it is unlikely to end with "Now I know what you mean by that."

🌹

When men argue with their wives, words often flail them.

The only way for a husband to get the last word is to apologise!

A husband is a man who stands by his wife through all the troubles she wouldn't have had, had she remained single!

A husband is the enigma who copes admirably with the intricacies of income tax and insurance, but who can never find his car keys or glasses.

A man walking in a Glasgow cemetery came across a chap prostrate across a grave, crying uncontrollably and shouting, "Why did you go? Why did you leave?" The man sympathises and asks if it was the grave of a dear friend or relative. "No," said the man. "It was the wife's first husband."

Arriving home from work, a man was greeted by his wife. "I have got good news for you and bad news." He swallowed hard and said he would like the good news first. "The air-bag in the car works."

❧

Marriage has been defined as a process where a man finds out what sort of guy his wife would have preferred

❧

A husband who had been waiting very patiently for his wife, finally shouted up to her, "Are you ready yet?" Back came the reply, "I've been telling you for half-an hour that I will be ready in a minute."

"When I get married", said a daughter to her mother, "I am going to invite all my friends to a lavish dinner with the best champagne, and I am going to have the whole thing video recorded." When her mother asked her if she had told her father about the kind of wedding she wanted, the daughter said, "No." "Well," said her mother, "let me know when you do tell him, because I would like to video-record that!"

❧

An American married to an Englishwoman tells how, shortly after their wedding, they paid a visit to New York. When the plane landed, she headed with her British passport to the foreigners' queue, while he headed for the American passport line. When the immigration officer asked her the purpose of her trip, she replied, "Pleasure. I am on my honeymoon." The officer looked first to one side of her, then the other. "Interesting," he said as he stamped her passport. "Most women on their honeymoon bring their husband with them."

A reluctant husband found himself volunteered by his wife as a fourth at bridge. He managed, however, to extricate himself rather swiftly by looking at his hand and muttering, "Let's see what I have got here ... a ten of valentines, a king of clovers, a gardening ace and a ..."

Husbands can be a bit slow on the uptake. A Glasgow Mum was tidying out a drawer and found a picture of her taken 20 years earlier standing in front of the family car in a T-shirt and shorts. She thought to herself that she was a pretty hot babe in those days. Showing the photo to her husband she asked "What do you think?" "Our old Cortina!" he foolishly replied.

Late shoppers were frantically completing their Christmas shopping. The roads were filled with cars, the pavements packed with people. At one corner a middle-aged couple were waiting to cross the road. The husband was loaded with parcels. "Get back to the pavement, George!" his wife shouted as he inched his way out on to the street. But he paid no attention. Finally, in a voice that almost drowned out the traffic noise, she screamed, "If you are not going to wait until it is clear to cross, let me have the parcels!"

An obituary in the local paper stated that the deceased "was 80 years old at the time of his death, and had been married for 59 years and nine months. His ordeal is over."

Makeovers

Makeovers are all the rage these days. Sometimes a new hairstyle or hair colour, or a new outfit can bring a smile to people's faces and make them feel like a new person. For others the makeover sometimes involves much more. To try and improve their appearance, some will undergo surgical procedures which are expensive and sometimes painful.

I have never had a desire to undergo a surgical procedure in the hope of improving my less than perfect physique and looks. But there have been times when I wished that I could get the kind of makeover that would make me a better person, that would suppress my ego-centricity, that would make it easier for me to rejoice when someone else excelled where I had failed, or achieved the promotion I longed for, that would eliminate false pride. Too often 'the good that I would, I do not'.

Once a year we enjoy Dickens' story about Scrooge, a very unattractive businessman being made over by the visits of three ghosts into a genial, almost saintly old man. I believe this Christmas story has stayed alive for almost two hundred years because, even in cynical and irreligious human beings, there is from time to time an unacknowledged longing to be a better person.

The laws of logic and simple arithmetic might lead us to think that giving ourselves away in service to others will mean that we end up with less of ourselves than we had to begin with. But in fact the reverse is true, logic and arithmetic go hang! A life wrapped up in itself is a very small package. We grow in stature by our interactive involvement with others. The door to real happiness opens outwards. We find our own good in the common good. Linking ourselves to something beyond the narrow ambit of self-interest – kindnesses rendered, help given, understanding shown – not only changes the lives of others, but can change us for the better.

Those who fail to realise this, who lose the stimulus of feeling useful or doing something which they know to be worthwhile, are tobogganed into ripe old age before they are sixty. Helena Rubenstein the beauty expert once said, "I have never had my face lifted. I prefer to have my spirits lifted. The effect of the latter is greater and more lasting than the former." Hollywood is one of the few places where they take you at face-lifted value.

Mungo McInnes

Lord Ballantrae once told how, in the Ayrshire village of Ballantrae, there lived a retired man called Mungo McInnes. He was not only big of stature but had a large white beard. Mungo, who had been a forester all his life, was idolised by the local children. He told them the most fantastic stories about how once, when shipwrecked on a desert island, he had fought and killed a bear. In another of his amazing stories he told the village youngsters how the ship on which he was sailing had been attacked by pirates. The children sat enthralled, believing everything Mungo told them.

When Lord Ballantrae's wife, who taught the infants in the local Sunday school began her lesson one Sunday by asking the children, "Who made the world?" one wee lad asked if it was Mungo McInnes! Meeting Mungo on the street the following day, she told him what had happened, how when she had asked the children who had made the world, one wee lad had asked "Was it Mungo McInnes?" On hearing this Mungo stroked his beard and said, "Well I suppose I did have a hand in it."

Mungo's answer was perhaps not as far-fetched as it sounds. We all have a hand in making the world the kind of world it is. We are all in a sense living in the 8th day of creation.

Connectors

Rabbi Jeffrey Salkin once told how a young New York taxi driver drove him to the airport. On the journey the young man informed him that though as a boy he had regularly attended the synagogue, he had not done so since his bar mitzvah. He then asked the Rabbi what he would say to a Jew like him.

Recalling that in Jewish folklore the *baal aqalah*, (the wagon driver) was an honoured profession, Rabbi Salkin suggested that they might begin by talking about his work. Surprised at hearing this, the young driver asked what his work had to do with religion. In reply the Rabbi pointed out that he was not only a taxi-driver, but a piece of the tissue that connects all humanity. He then went on to explain what he meant by that. He told him that from the airport he was flying to a different city. There he would give a couple of lectures that might change the life of someone present. Just by driving him to the airport he was making that connection possible. Having heard on the two-way taxi radio that after he dropped him, he was going to pick up a woman from the hospital, Rabbi Salkin pointed out that he, being the first non-medical person she would encounter after being in hospital, could be a small part of her healing process, an agent of her re-entry into the world of health. After that, the Rabbi said, he might pick up someone from the station who was returning home from seeing a dying parent. If that happened, his friendly sympathetic voice could be a source of comfort.

The Rabbi's aim was to try and get the young taxi-driver to see that he was a connector, a bridge builder, one of the many unseen people who make the world work as well as it does, that his role in life was not just an important one, but a sacred one.

Whatever the nature of our work, by our meeting and speaking to people, we can all inspire nobler living in others, and bring a little more love into the world. I warm to the Buddhist saying, "No seed ever sees the flower". Though in our interconnected world, our kindly actions and words can have a wide impact, we will often know nothing of that impact.

Remembering

Memory bridges seas and continents quicker than light. It is like a winter garden in which the seeds of the past lie dormant, ready to spring again into bloom. It is a time machine which enables us to think and feel our way back through time. Though in one sense the past is over and done with, in another sense it is not done with at all.

There are three phases to the process of remembering – registration, consolidation and retrieval. Diseases like Alzheimer's, which affect the second and third phases, greatly impoverish life. Though many aspects of the human memory are a great mystery, what is clear is that the oftener we recall a memory, the more permanent it becomes.

Unfortunately some unhappy people have too good a memory for the wrong things, for every slight, real or imaginary. They keep stirring up unhappy memories like a witch's potion, regularly adding new grievances. Such constant retelling results in their grudges festering. How different it was with Abraham Lincoln. We are told he never remembered a wrong done to him, and never forgot a kindness. What a consecrated use of memory.

Fond memories are a second chance at happiness – memories of glad and gracious things that happened to us, memories of special family holidays, of parents, teachers and friends who helped shape and enrich our lives. Though my mother died when I was a teenager, she will always be part of who I am. By means of memory I can still see her face, and hear her bedtime stories about the pupils with special needs in the Hamilton school where in the 1920s she was headmistress. I also recall with great fondness hours in life when I became more aware that there is a goodness and sacredness about life, deeper than all its shabbiness and horror. What a blessing such memories are.